Bruce Byfield

Styles and Templates

Designing with LibreOffice, Extract 1

Editor & Publisher

Jean Hollis Weber, Friends of OpenDocument, Inc., 544 Carlyle Gardens, Beck Drive North, Condon, Queensland 4815, Australia. Please direct any comments or suggestions about this document to info@friendsofopendocument.com.

Reviewers

Jean Hollis Weber, Lee Schlesinger, Nicola Einarson, Terry Hancock, Charlie Kravetz, Michael Manning, Jean-Francois Nifenecker, Georges Rodier, Christina Teskey.

Special thanks also go to Marcel Gagné, Michael Meeks, and Carla Schroder for advanced reading.

Acknowledgments

Parts of this book's content were originally published, sometimes in different forms, by Linux Journal, Linux.com, Linux Pro Magazine, Open Content and Software, Wazi, and WorldLabel. My thanks for permission to re-use this material.

Publication date and software version

Published 15 September 2016. Based on LibreOffice Version 5.0.2.2 and later.

Photo credits

Cover photos and the photo on the interior title page are copyright by Bruce Byfield and released under the Creative Commons Attribution Sharealike License, version 3.0 or later.

They depict the Sun Yat Sen Classical Garden in Vancouver, Canada. The gardens are based on the philosophy of feng shui, which, like typography, works deliberately to produce a natural, unnoticed effect. All photos are used with permission.

Table of Contents

Chapter 3

Chapter 4

For Trish, Always

1

Introduction

This book is an extract from a much larger book entitled *Designing with LibreOffice*. It is intended for those who only want information on how to use styles and templates in LibreOffice, the popular free-licensed office suite. It consists of Chapter 2, 3 and 11 in the larger book.

Eventually, this book will be the first of five extracts. Currently, however, only the first two extracts have been released.

The excerpts will be:

Part 1: Styles and Templates
Part 2: Choosing Fonts
Part 3: Character and Paragraph Styles
Part 4: Page, Frame, and List Styles
Part 5: Slide Shows, Diagrams, and Spreadsheets

The emphasis in each book is design. In all of them, design is defined, not as formatting that calls attention to itself, like an HTML blink tag, but as formatting that is attractive and makes a document easy to read, edit, and maintain.

Together, the five smaller books will contain most, but not all the information from the larger book. Any changes are minimal, and made for continuity or changes in structure made necessary by the changes in format.

Tip

You can download the entire *Designing with LibreOffice* book or other excerpts (when available) from:

http://designingwithlibreoffice.com/download-buy/

Printed versions of the entire book or of excerpts (when available) are for sale at the Friends of Open Document store at:

http://www.lulu.com/spotlight/opendocument

If you need information on features or selections that are not mentioned in this book, see the LibreOffice documentation page:

http://www.libreoffice.org/get-help/documentation/

Printed versions of the LibreOffice manuals are also available for sale at the Friends of Open Document store:

http://www.lulu.com/spotlight/opendocument

2

Going in style

You have two ways to design a document in LibreOffice: by manual formatting and by applying styles. Or, as I like to joke: the wrong way and the right way.

Manual formatting (also called direct formatting) is how most people design a document. When you format manually, whenever you want to change the default formatting, you select part of the document – for example, a paragraph or a page – and then apply the formatting using the tool bars or one of the menus.

Then you do the same thing all over again in the next place that you want the same formatting. And the next, and the next.

If you decide to change the formatting, you have to go through the entire document, changing the design one place at a time.

Manual formatting is popular because it requires little knowledge of the software. In effect, you are using the office application as though it were a typewriter.

But although this approach gets the job done, it's slow. Not only that, but many features are awkward to use when you format manually – assuming you can use them at all.

By contrast, a style is a set of formats. For example, a character style might put characters into italics if they form the title of the book. A page style might list everything about how a page is designed, from the width of its margins to its orientation and the background color.

The advantage of styles is that you design everything once. Instead of adding all the characteristics every place where you format, you apply the style.

If you decide you want a different format, you edit the style once, and within seconds, every place where you applied the style has the new format as well.

You don't have to remember the details of the formatting, either – just the name of the style.

Example: Formatting with styles

To fully appreciate the difference between formatting manually and formatting with styles, imagine that you are preparing a twenty page essay for a university class. You have decided to use the DejaVu Serif typeface with a size of 10 points. Twenty minutes before you leave for class, you re-read the professor's instructions and realize that she only accepts essays in 12 point Times New Roman.

If you have manually formatted, you will be lucky to finish editing before you leave. But if you have used styles, you can change the font and its size in less than a minute, and print out a new copy of the essay with time to spare.

Then you can save the document as a template. The next essay you write for that professor, you can concentrate on content and not have to worry about formatting.

Other advantages of styles? You can mostly eliminate the need for tabs, especially at the start of a new paragraph, because you can create a style that automatically indents for you.

Similarly, instead of creating a separate frame for a section formatted differently from the rest of the document, you can include the different format in a set of styles and keep typing.

Another major advantage is that if you use heading styles, you can use them as bookmarks in Navigator to help you move around in a document. But unlike normal bookmarks, you don't have to define them in a separate task. Instead, headings are available for use the moment that you set the styles.

In the same way, headings let you generate a table of contents with a minimum of settings. Separate headers and footers for different pages are easier to maintain. You can give a uniform look to the frames around photos you add, set up a drop capital to mark the start of a new chapter, and automatically change page layouts, freeing yourself to focus on content.

However, the real saving comes when you save your design as a template. Once you have created your basic templates, the next time you start a document, you won't have to think about formatting at all – instead, you can open the template and start writing. Usually, the more you use styles, the more time you save.

Amazingly, some users view styles as an intrusion on their rights to work as they please. Of course they can do as they like, but not using styles means they work harder than necessary.

Debunking myths about styles

People who have never used styles often have bizarre ideas about them. Sometimes, these ideas may be excuses to rationalize not using styles, but often they are misunderstandings.

Here are some of the most common myths about styles that are repeated whenever the subject of manual formatting vs. styles is discussed:

Myth about styles	Reality
• Styles impose on users' right to work the way they choose.	• You can work without styles. But why demand the right to inconvenience yourself?
• Styles are hard to learn.	• Styles represent a different way of thinking than manual formatting. However, you can learn their basic concepts in ten minutes.
• Styles are for programmers, not ordinary users.	• Styles are for anybody who wants to work efficiently. Actually, just as many programmers format manually as anyone else.
• Styles require you to memorize their names.	• You don't need to memorize anything. You just need to read from the lists of styles in LibreOffice.
• What you set in styles applies to all the document, so styles more limited than manual formatting.	• A style affects only the parts of a document to which you apply it.
• Styles are too complicated.	• You don't need to understand every feature of every style. Often, you can just accept the defaults.

- Styles are limiting. You can't change what's built into them.

- Most aspects of styles can be fine-tuned, toggled on or off, or ignored until you need them. You can't do anything manually that you can't do with styles much more easily.

- Styles can conflict with each other.

- Only one style of a particular type can apply to a selection. You can have a character and a paragraph style applying to the same selection, but not two different character styles or two different paragraph styles.

- Manual formatting is preferable because you can make changes on the fly.

- You can change styles on the fly, too. In fact, changing styles is quicker; you only have to make a change once to apply it through the entire document.

Example: Styles save time

Just how much time do you save by using styles? Let's imagine that you have a heading paragraph that you want to format extensively.

Specifically, you want to set the font, font size, font weight, font color, and the space above the paragraph. In addition, you want to edit the heading so that it starts with a number.

The shortest way to make these changes manually is:

Steps	Action
1	Highlight the text of the header.
2–4	Open the font list in the tool bar, scroll, and select the font.
5–6	Open the font size in the tool bar, scroll, and select the font size.
7	Select font weight from the tool bar icon.
8–9	Open FONT COLOR in the tool bar and select the color.
10–14	Select from the menu FORMAT > PARAGRAPH > INDENTS & SPACING, edit the SPACE ABOVE field, and click OK.
15	Add a numbered list from the tool bar.

If you are lucky, you might save a few actions if you don't have to scroll for a setting, but this series of steps is a good average. You would have to repeat these steps, of course, for every header in the document.

By contrast, setting up a style would take 21 steps. Once the style is ready, here's how you would make the same changes using styles:

Steps	Action
1	Place the cursor anywhere in the header paragraph.
2	Press F11 to open the STYLES AND FORMATTING floating window.

3   Change the display in STYLES AND FORMATTING to ALL STYLES (or another view that shows the style you want).

4   Scroll to the paragraph style you want.

5   Select the paragraph style.

This example is extremely conservative. If you are using styles, then probably the STYLES AND FORMATTING window is already open. Often, too, you may not need to change the view.

However, even being conservative, applying the style requires one-third the number of actions than making the changes manually. When you change one paragraph's style, you also change every other use of the style in the same document. That means that if the document has more than two instances of the heading, using styles saves you effort.

When should you use styles?

The short answer is, "Whenever it saves time." Still, in practice, even experts sometimes use manual formatting in certain circumstances.

Format manually if:	Use styles if:
• The document is short (1-2 pages), and you have no templates that you can use.	• The document is long (over 3 pages).
• The document will be used once and never reused.	• The document is going to be used over and over.

- The document will only be edited by a single person.

- The document will be edited by more than one person.

- Any editing will only take place within a few days of finishing the document.

- The document will be edited weeks, months, or even years after the first version.

- Some people who will edit the document have no idea how to use styles, and refuse to learn.

- The document belongs to a standard class of documents, such as a letter, a fax, or memo.

- A consistent format doesn't matter for some other reason. For example, the document is informal, and won't affect your company's branding.

- The document design must match that of other documents from you or your company or organization.

- You are experimenting with styles while building a template. Until you finalize the styles, you will make so many changes that creating styles is mostly wasted effort.

- You want to use the document in a number of different ways, each of which requires some minor changes: for example, printing it on both a white and a red background.

- The document's formatting is extremely simple and regular, like an essay.

- The document is highly formatted, like a brochure.

The more circumstances that apply, the clearer your decision.

However, even if all indications are to use manual formatting, you may find a template you can re-use.

The types of styles

Most office suites have paragraph and character styles in their word processors. However, LibreOffice adds three more styles in Writer (plus a still being implemented style for tables), as well as other styles for spreadsheets, presentations, and diagrams.

The additional styles make Writer less a word processor and more of an intermediate desktop publishing tool. Writer may lack the precision of a tool like InDesign, but it compares favorably with a tool like FrameMaker for text-heavy documents. In fact, some publishers prefer to use Writer for designing their books.

Admittedly, styles are less useful in other applications. However, in these other applications, styles do help to centralize frequently used settings, which is a benefit by itself.

The styles available are:

Style	Comment
Writer	
PARAGRAPH	PARAGRAPH styles are the most commonly used style. A paragraph begins and ends when you press the ENTER key. Common paragraph styles include those for body text and headings. Equivalent to manual formatting with FORMAT > PARAGRAPH, plus some extras.

CHARACTER	CHARACTER styles modify selected letters in a paragraph style. Common character styles are bold lettering for emphasis, italics for a book title, and underlining and a different color for a web link. An exact equivalent to manual formatting with FORMAT > CHARACTER.
FRAME	All objects inserted to a Writer document are contained by a frame. By customizing FRAME styles, you can automatically adjust elements such as the border around objects and how text flows around them. Right-click on a selected frame for the manual equivalent.
PAGE	PAGE styles are the most reliable way to format pages differently, including headers and footers and footnotes. The main drawback is that you cannot easily set an object to reoccur on every page that uses the same page style. Exact equivalent to manual formatting with FORMAT > PAGE.
LIST	Styles for configuring bullet lists and numbered lists. LIST styles can be applied directly to a list, or, more elegantly, associated with one or more paragraph styles. Equivalent to manually formatting with FORMAT > BULLETS AND NUMBERING.

Styles and Templates

TABLES	Table styles are being slowly implemented, starting with the 5.3 release. For now, you can save and apply table designs by selecting TABLE > AUTOFORMAT > ADD.

Calc

CELL	CELL styles set both the appearance of cells and the types of content in them, such as percentages or currency. They also can automatically set the number of decimal places used by the cell, and automatically wrap and hyphenate the contents of a style.
PAGE	PAGE styles set how to arrange selected sheets or cells to print to paper.

Draw & Impress

GRAPHIC	Styles for drawing objects, including graphic text.
PRESENTATION	Styles for the contents of slides (Impress).

Working with styles

To open the STYLES AND FORMATTING window, do one of the following:

- Select FORMAT > STYLES AND FORMATTING from the menu bar.
- Press the F11 key.
- Click the MORE... link at the bottom of the style list in the FORMATTING tool bar.
- Select the STYLES AND FORMATTING button on the sidebar.

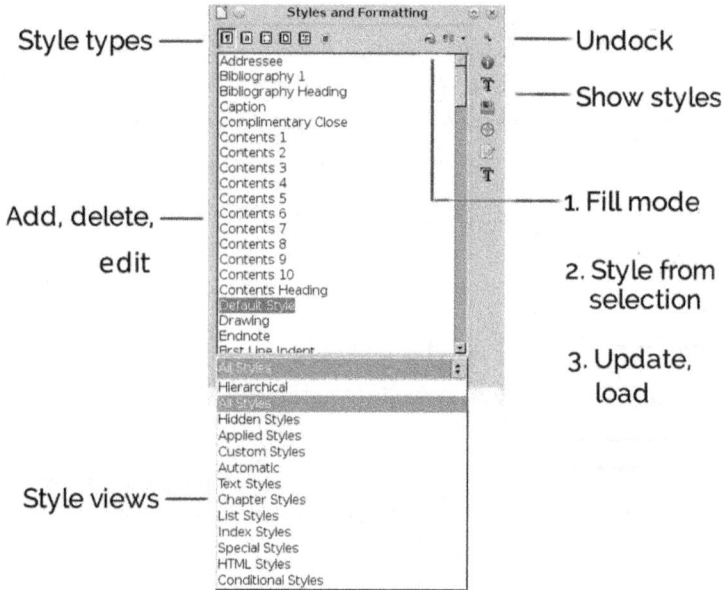

Style types —

Add, delete, —

edit

Style views —

— Undock

— Show styles

1. Fill mode

2. Style from selection

3. Update, load

Writer's version of the STYLES AND FORMATTING window.

Undocking the Styles and Formatting window

Until LibreOffice version 4.4, the STYLES AND FORMATTING window opened as a floating window. The floating window could be placed anywhere on the screen, or dragged to be docked on either side of the editing window. However, starting in version 4.4, it opens in the sidebar.

To undock the window (or any other display in the sidebar), click the drop-down list of commands on the top right of the tool bar and select UNDOCK. When the window is undocked, select DOCK from the drop-down list to redock it. LibreOffice remembers whether the window is docked or undocked when you restart it.

Tip

The sidebar remains undocked, even after you exit and restart LibreOffice.

In OpenOffice and many earlier LibreOffice versions, drag the floating window by its title bar to the left or right edge of the editing window. When a frame appears, release the floating window, and it is docked. Dragging on the title bar of the docked window should undock it, although the reliability of the feature varies with the release.

Changing the style type

On the top left of the window are icons for each type of style. If you hover the mouse over them, you will see what type of style each icon represents. Click an icon to display the styles for its particular type.

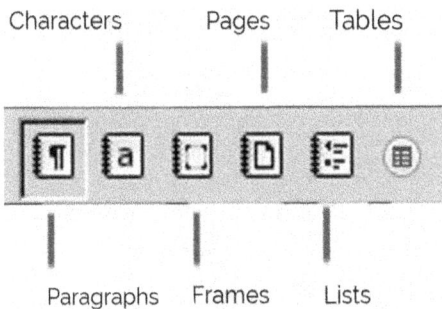

Characters   Pages   Tables

Paragraphs   Frames   Lists

The types of styles in Writer. Paragraph styles are selected.

Viewing styles

Because the list of styles is long, the drop-down list at the bottom of the window has filtered views that need less scrolling.

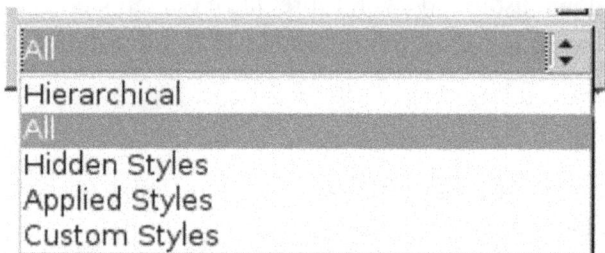

All ▲▼
Hierarchical
All
Hidden Styles
Applied Styles
Custom Styles

Style views filter the styles that display.

The best view depends on what you are doing. For example, when you are designing, the HIERARCHICAL view helps you work with related styles. By contrast, after you have written a few pages, the APPLIED STYLES view minimizes the styles displayed.

The basic views vary with the application. The most common ones are:

- HIERARCHICAL: Shows how styles are related to each other (See "The hierarchy of styles," page 27). Helps you decide where to make changes in multiple styles by editing just one of them.

- APPLIED STYLES: The styles used in the current document. This view is useless with a new document, but as you continue to work, it reduces the number of styles displayed.

- CUSTOM STYLES: The styles you have created, as opposed to the pre-defined ones.

- AUTOMATIC: A minimalist list of pre-defined styles. AUTOMATIC is the default view when you open a new document.

- ALL STYLES: Especially when you are viewing paragraph styles, the ALL STYLES view can give you so many names to scan that using it is counter-productive. Use ALL STYLES only when you are completely unable to find the style you want.

- HIDDEN STYLES: Styles you have removed from the other views to reduce the clutter.

Paragraph styles have a number of additional views. Most are self-explanatory divisions of the uses for styles, such as HTML STYLES and INDEX STYLES.

Styles that don't fit into any other category, such as CAPTION, FOOTER LEFT, or TABLE CONTENTS are listed as SPECIAL STYLES.

Tip

The HTML view shows the paragraph styles that LibreOffice has mapped directly to specific HTML tags.

Finding current styles

The STYLES AND FORMATTING window always opens with the style for the current cursor position highlighted. If you change the type of style displayed in the STYLES AND FORMATTING window, then the highlighted style also changes, if possible.

For example, if you are using the TEXT BODY paragraph style and switch the display to character styles, ordinarily the DEFAULT STYLE will be highlighted. However, if you switch to the list styles, nothing will be highlighted unless the cursor is at a position where a list style is being used.

In Writer, you can identify current styles in other places in the editing window. When closed, the list of paragraph styles on the FORMATTING tool bar always displays the current style.

Similarly, the current page style is shown, third from the left, in the indicators at the bottom of the editing window. As you scroll through a document, it is updated automatically.

In addition, you can select EDIT > FIND & REPLACE > OTHER OPTIONS > SEARCH FOR PARAGRAPH STYLES to locate where a style is used in a document. Finding character styles is not directly possible, but FIND & REPLACE's OTHER OPTIONS do include search by settings of character styles using ATTRIBUTES and FORMAT.

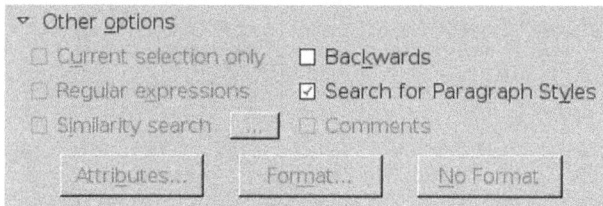

SEARCH FOR PARAGRAPH STYLES is an essential option for editing format and structure.

The nature of styles

LibreOffice has pre-defined styles that you can modify but not delete. In each style type, especially paragraph and character styles, the pre-defined styles are well thought out, and might be all that you need. In fact, one school of thought holds that you have less trouble if you use only pre-defined styles, even though that may limit your designs. Whether that is true is uncertain, but the pre-defined styles are useful references for what you can do with styles.

In addition, you can create custom styles that are based on pre-defined ones, or entirely new ones by clicking on any pre-defined style. Custom styles provide the specialized needs that the pre-defined styles do not.

Both custom and pre-defined styles behave similarly. Understanding their behaviors is essential for working with all styles.

The hierarchy of styles

Many styles in LibreOffice are hierarchical (although for some reason a few, such as LIST styles, are not). In other words, they are ordered in a tree, with each style taking its characteristics from the one at the top and modifying some of them.

A style that is one level above another is called the parent of the style directly below it. Similarly, styles that are one level below another one are called its children. Changing a parent style also changes its children.

This relationship can be confusing, especially the first time a style apparently changes its characteristics spontaneously. However, by making changes to the parent, you save the time you would spend changing its children one at a time.

```
▽Heading
    Bibliography Heading
    Contents Heading
    Heading 1
    Heading 2
    Heading 3
    Heading 4
    Heading 5
    Heading 6
    Heading 7
    Heading 8
    Heading 9
    Heading 10
```

A style hierarchy for paragraph styles in Writer. Changes to the HEADING style will change all the styles below it.

Changing the style hierarchy

You can manipulate the style hierarchy using the INHERIT FROM field on the ORGANIZER tab. The style inherited from is the current style's parent – the style from which the current style inherits characteristics.

> **Tip**
>
> In Apache OpenOffice and earlier LibreOffice releases, the INHERIT FROM field is called LINKED WITH.

Sometimes, you may want to use the field to set an arbitrary parent. For example, if you created two paragraph styles for bullets, differing only in the list style each used, you could save time by setting one of the styles as the parent of another. Either one would do – the point is to make changes only once, not twice.

The Default styles

The only styles that do not have a hierarchical parent are those at the top of the entire tree. In paragraph and character styles, this style is called DEFAULT. All other styles of the same type are based upon the DEFAULT style.

You can choose to edit the DEFAULT style so that it includes the basic formatting you have chosen for the document. Alternatively, you can leave the DEFAULT style unchanged, so that you can exchange documents easily with people on other machines.

This second choice is not always possible because different versions of LibreOffice may set different DEFAULT styles, but is worth trying. In effect, this approach uses another style such as TEXT BODY as an unofficial default, leaving the DEFAULT style to function like FORMAT > CLEAR DIRECT FORMATTING.

Either way, the DEFAULT styles are useful when pasting formatted text from inside or outside the current document creates formatting problems.

The easiest way to solve these problems is to strip out most of the formatting by applying the DEFAULT character and/or paragraph style, then to apply the formatting you want.

Tip

Lists sometimes leave bullets or numbers behind after you apply the default paragraph style to them. When that happens, press the BACKSPACE key until the bullet or number disappears.

The Organizer tab

The window for each style throughout LibreOffice is divided into tabs. Many tabs, such as the BORDER and the AREA tabs, display identical features throughout LibreOffice; so, in later chapters, the book gives cross-references to prevent repetition.

Of all the tabs, the ORGANIZER tab is most important. It summarizes the style and its relation to other styles.

The ORGANIZER tab can include four fields:

- NAME: The entry that appears in the STYLE AND FORMATTING window. It should be descriptive or suggest the style's function.

- NEXT STYLE: The style that is automatically used next when you press the ENTER key. For instance, HEADING 1 is often followed by TEXT BODY. Since a heading is almost never followed immediately by another heading, this is a reasonable choice. By contrast, TEXT BODY's NEXT STYLE is usually TEXT BODY, because several paragraphs in a row are likely to be text.

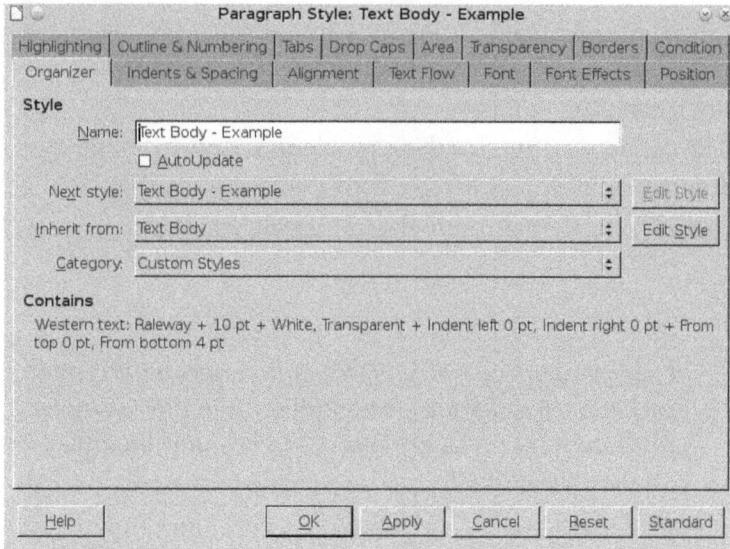

To change a style's parent, change the INHERIT FROM field on the ORGANIZER tab (may be called LINKED WITH).

- INHERIT FROM (LINKED WITH): The parent style in the hierarchy. Changes to the parent style will change the current style, so you don't have to make changes to every related style.
- CATEGORY: The view in which the style is listed. By default, styles you create are displayed in CUSTOM STYLES, but you can choose any other view instead.

Tip

You can sometimes make a view more effective by changing which category each of your custom styles displays in.

In addition, the ORGANIZER tab shows a summary of all the formatting options selected for the style, similar to the one that WordPerfect gives.

The fields in the ORGANIZER tab are grayed-out in types of styles where they would make no sense. For example, two frames seldom occur one after the other, so a FRAME style window omits the NEXT STYLE category. Similarly, the CATEGORY field is grayed out, because only one view is necessary for frames.

Applying styles

To apply a style, you must select part of the document. A paragraph or page is selected when the mouse cursor is anywhere in or on them, but frames or drawing objects must be selected by clicking in them so the frame and its eight handles displays. You can also drag the mouse to select multiple paragraphs or spreadsheet cells.

You have several options for applying a style: the STYLES AND FORMATTING window, the FORMATTING tool bar, FILL FORMAT mode, pasting from your system's clipboard, and applying keyboard shortcuts.

Using the Styles and Formatting window

With the STYLES AND FORMATTING window open, you can apply a style with a single mouse-click – or maybe two as you select another style category to list.

For many users, the STYLES AND FORMATTING window is the most efficient way to apply styles. Some users keep it docked in the sidebar, which can mean that a maximized window is necessary, depending on the size of your monitor.

If you prefer not to work in maximized windows, undock the window and place it where it is close enough to the editing window to minimize mouse motions, but far enough away that it doesn't block what you are doing.

Starting with version 5.0, the STYLES AND FORMATTING window shows a preview of the current font formatting. This preview is useful when dealing with character styles, but omits most of the information in a paragraph or a list style. With frame and page styles, it is mostly a distraction.

Using the Formatting tool bar

In Writer, you can apply paragraph styles to a selection by opening the drop-down list of styles that is on the left on the FORMATTING tool bar (the default bottom tool bar).

Tip

When applying a style, always click on the left of a list item. Otherwise, you risk being entangled in the menu.

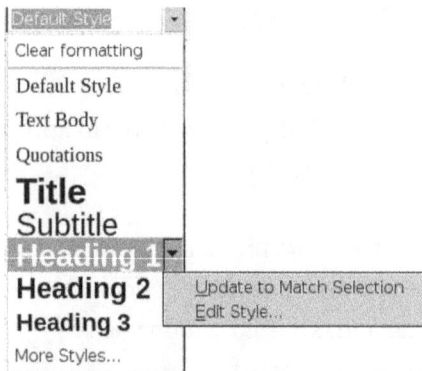

Default Style
Clear formatting
Default Style
Text Body
Quotations
Title
Subtitle
Heading 1
Heading 2   Update to Match Selection
Heading 3   Edit Style...
More Styles...

The styles list in the FORMATTING toolbar.

When you first open a document, the list includes only a half dozen commonly used styles. Gradually, though, other paragraph styles are listed as they are used in the document. Clicking the MORE STYLES... link at the bottom of the list opens the STYLES AND FORMATTING window, while selecting EDIT STYLE from a style's drop-down menu opens the dialog window for the style.

Similarly, UPDATE TO MATCH SELECTION edits the style based on the formatting of the text you select before opening the drop-down list.

The list has the advantage of offering a preview of each paragraph style. Unfortunately, that preview is only the name of the style, which means that many formatting elements are not shown in the preview.

Consequently, the list is a limited tool at best. At most it serves as a reminder of what the style looks like.

Using Fill Format Mode

With the STYLES AND FORMATTING window, you also have the option with some style categories of reversing the basic application technique, choosing the style first, and where to apply it second. When applying character styles, it is almost like painting with the cursor, as its icon in the STYLES AND FORMATTING window suggests.

To use FILL FORMAT:

1   Select a style.

2   Click the FILL FORMAT MODE button (the second from the right at the top of the STYLES AND FORMATTING window).

When FILL FORMAT is available, the cursor changes to a paint bucket.

If the button is grayed out, you cannot use FILL FORMAT with the style category selected.

3 Drag the cursor over the part of the document you wish to format. You need to drag the cursor for only a few characters to apply the style to a paragraph or a page. However, to apply a character style, you need to drag the cursor across all the characters you plan to format.

4 Click the FILL FORMAT MODE button a second time to turn the mode off.

STOP
Caution
Right-clicking anywhere in a document when FILL FORMAT MODE is turned on stops it from being applied.

Pasting styles

The rules for copying and pasting styles are simple regardless of whether you use PASTE or PASTE SPECIAL, or are copying from one document to another:

* When source material formatted in a style with the same name as a style in the target is copied into a paragraph, then the target's style is used.

* When source material formatted in a style not in the target is copied into a new paragraph, then the formatting is kept and the style name is added to the target document.

* Any formatting done manually or with a character style in the source is copied wherever it is pasted.

These rules hold true for all types of styles.

They also hold true for any Open Document Format file, including those created in Apache OpenOffice or Calligra Suite, the free office program designed for the KDE desktop.

You can remove most of this formatting by selecting CLEAR FORMATTING from the top of the drop-down list of paragraph styles on the FORMATTING tool bar.

Unfortunately, some of the original formatting, including the text color and any underlining, sometimes remains when available system memory is low. When it does, applying the DEFAULT character style may remove it. If some formatting still persists, retype the material.

Tip

When you paste material, click the arrow beside the PASTE icon in the top toolbar and select UNFORMATTED TEXT. The extra step may prevent formatting difficulties.

Applying styles using keyboard shortcuts

Pressing CTRL+1 ... CTRL+5 applies the HEADING 1-5 styles. These shortcuts can be useful in documents such as an outline, in which you are using only Heading paragraph styles. You can set keyboard shortcuts for other styles from TOOLS > CUSTOMIZE > FUNCTIONS > STYLES.

Keyboard shortcuts can save stress on your wrists and hands when you are typing for long periods, so you may want to record additional macros and assign them to keyboard shortcuts. The DEFAULT STYLE and TEXT BODY paragraph styles are likely candidates for macros, and so are the EMPHASIS and STRONG EMPHASIS character styles.

STOP Caution

To record macros in LibreOffice, you first need to select TOOLS > OPTIONS > LIBREOFFICE > ADVANCED > ENABLE MACRO RECORDING (LIMITED). The menu item RECORD MACRO is then listed under TOOLS > MACROS without any need to re-start LibreOffice.

Creating and modifying styles

LibreOffice has styles for most ordinary purposes, so one way to save time is to use only pre-defined styles, changing no more attributes than necessary. On the whole, the styles have intelligent defaults, and you usually only have to make a few changes while designing.

However, if you decide to edit styles, you have several options in Writer:

- Right-click on a style in the STYLES AND FORMATTING window and select NEW to create a style that clones the selected style (in other words, one that is a child of the selected style in the hierarchy). Be sure to rename it immediately. If you forget to rename, you can find the new style at the bottom of the list of styles, named something like UNTITLED1.

- Right-click on a style in the STYLES AND FORMATTING window and select MODIFY to edit the selected style.

- Manually format and select part of the document. Open the drop-down list on the top right of the STYLES AND FORMATTING window and select NEW Style from Selection. This option is handy for creating styles on-the-fly or if you have a hard time visualizing settings while you are planning a design.

- Select a passage and drag it to the STYLES AND FORMATTING window when it displays paragraph or character styles. A dialog window opens so that you can give the new style a title.

- Select the AUTOUPDATE check box on the ORGANIZER tab of a style. When this box is selected, any manual formatting you do automatically updates the style.

- Edit styles from the tool bar. In LibreOffice 4.4 and later, you can update styles by highlighting part of the document, then selecting a style in the tool bar's drop-down list and clicking UPDATE TO MATCH SELECTION.

STOP Caution

Only select AUTOUPDATE if everyone editing the document uses styles. Otherwise, the result could be stylistic chaos. In fact, when using styles, discourage any editors from doing any manual formatting.

You also have the option of copying styles from a template into the current document. See "Changing templates," page 64.

Tip

LibreOffice usually updates its styles in a matter of seconds. However, if you make enough changes quickly enough, it may fail to keep up, especially on machines with minimal memory.

If problems continue, try selecting UPDATE STYLE from the drop-down list on the right of the STYLES AND FORMATTING window after working on each style. If you continue to have problems, closing and reopening the document should solve it.

Hiding and deleting styles

Hiding styles reduces the clutter in the STYLES AND FORMATTING window. To hide a style, select HIDE from the right-click menu, one style at a time. If you need to use the style again, you can restore it from the HIDDEN STYLES view.

A custom style that is no longer needed can be deleted using the right-click menu. You cannot delete a pre-defined style. Styles installed from an extension can only be deleted by removing the extension in TOOLS > EXTENSION MANAGER.

STOP

Caution

LibreOffice warns that a style is in use, but does not stop you deleting it. The default style replaces a deleted one.

Naming styles

Especially in Writer, styles are named for their functions, followed by their position in the file hierarchy. For instance, USER INDEX1 is the paragraph style for the first level of text in an index. Similarly, character styles include EMPHASIS and INTERNET LINK.

Other names for pre-defined styles are descriptive, such as OBJECT WITHOUT FILL in Draw.

If you are working with multiple languages, keeping to the default style names avoids confusion. However, descriptive names can be easier to work with.

Tip

Since you will probably be using at least some pre-defined styles, you may decide to use the same conventions for custom styles.

However, to save yourself scrolling endlessly through the STYLES AND FORMATTING window, consider prefacing any custom styles with "C-" or some other unique preface. That way, you can easily find and apply custom styles without having to change the view.

In Writer, you sometimes find that you use different categories of styles in the same design. For example, a list style can have a character style associated with it so that you can have colored bullets or numbers. In addition, the same list style can be assigned to a paragraph style so that it is used whenever you choose the paragraph style. To help you find each of these styles later, give them the same name. Since each is in a different category, neither you nor LibreOffice should confuse them.

Automating style application

In most documents, some styles follow one another in a set pattern. A TITLE paragraph style is usually followed by a SUBTITLE, and a TEXT BODY paragraph style by another TEXT BODY. A FIRST PAGE style is usually followed by a LEFT PAGE, which is followed by a RIGHT PAGE.

You can take advantage of such patterns by filling in the NEXT STYLE field on the Organizer tab. With some types of styles, such as lists, having a NEXT STYLE makes no sense, and the field is grayed out. But with the NEXT STYLE field filled in, just starting a new paragraph or page will automatically apply the next style without your hands leaving the keyboard.

Another way of writing

Don't be surprised if you need time to get used to the idea of styles. Using styles involves more planning beforehand than manual formatting. Yet the basic concepts are straightforward, and already you might be starting to see how styles can automate formatting.

In the next chapter, you'll see how templates can help you recycle document designs to save you even more time.

3

Recycling using templates

No one has time to design a document every time they sit down to write. It's inefficient. Nor do you want everyone working on a project to design their own documents. The solution to both these problems is templates – files to store formatting and structure to re-use or share.

Templates are handled differently from ordinary documents. Before you use them, they need to be registered, so that LibreOffice is aware of them. They also have their own menus and menu items that normal files do not use.

Mostly, templates store formatting. However, they can also store structure, either in the form of outlines, or of fields that automatically fill in standard information or indicate with placeholders what kind of information should be added.

This structural use of templates tends to be under-emphasized. However, you can find examples of it in some releases of LibreOffice or OpenOffice in the Impress templates entitled "Introducing a New Strategy" and "Recommendation of a Strategy."

Both these templates include not only formatting, but a standard set of slides for developing a presentation with certain goals in mind. You can develop equally detailed structural templates to automate your work.

An Impress slide with a formal placeholder for the title and informal ones for other information. Placeholders help you to rough out a design without requiring specific information.

Tip

If you are a long-time user of office suites, you may be wary of templates because of how easily they became corrupted in Microsoft Word when you made any changes or tried to mix templates.

If so, don't worry. LibreOffice templates are designed to eliminate the problems that caused the corruption in Word. Mostly, they succeed, although sometimes at the cost of restricting what you can do with templates.

Styles and Templates

When to use templates

As with styles, the short answer is, "Whenever possible." Not only are templates more efficient than designing from scratch, but using them consistently helps you get used to the concepts behind them.

Over the years, I have heard users claim that templates are impractical because every document they do is different.

However, when I probe such claims, I usually find that the problem wasn't that every document was different, but that the person making the claims didn't think in terms of structure. Nor did they realize that a consistent general format can be part of corporate or personal branding.

A more plausible reason for not using templates is that setting them up takes time. Yet even that excuse fails to survive scrutiny.

Example

The all-purpose template I first designed in 2002 took several hours to design, and maybe another two to fine-tune.

Since then, I have used that all-purpose template for hundreds of documents. Each time I used it, I could start to write immediately and without worrying about how it was formatted.

At a minimum of three hours per template design, I have easily saved over a month's time thanks to that one template alone.

Other templates I have made over the years have seen less use. But always, the initial hours lost to template design have still been regained countless times over the years.

Using templates does mean planning ahead. But this new work flow rapidly repays the effort to change your work habits.

How templates work

Unlike Microsoft Word, LibreOffice does not display a NORMAL template anywhere in its menus. This omission eliminates the possibility of a document being corrupted by too much editing of the DEFAULT template.

The only way that you can alter LibreOffice's default formats without using templates is to change the font settings in TOOLS > OPTIONS > LIBREOFFICE WRITER > BASIC FONTS (WESTERN). Default formatting such as page and list styles cannot be edited at all.

However, you can also design a template with far more formatting information as default. Its settings will be used for every document when you select FILE > NEW, unless you specifically select another template.

Linking templates with documents

Whichever template you use, it must be properly registered before you can use it.

Only one template can be applied at one time to a document. This policy avoids the tendency to corruption that used to plague MS Word (and may still do, for all that I know).

STOP

Caution

Two styles of the same name in separate documents can have different formats.

If the template changes, the next time you restart LibreOffice and open the document, you are prompted to update the document. Styles shared by the template and the document are updated, but styles that are only in the document are not.

If you choose Update Styles, then the document continues to be linked to the template. However, remember to save the document after updating.

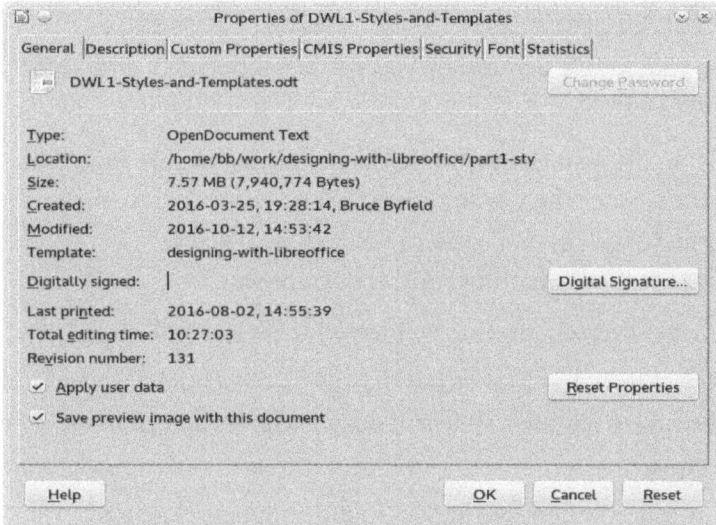

Files > Properties > General lists the template upon which the document was originally based. The layout of this tab is different in LibreOffice before release 4.3, with the template at the bottom of the window.

By contrast, if you choose Keep Old Styles, it is unlinked from the template, and you are not prompted for further updates when the template changes again. However, the Properties window continues to list the template, even though it is irrelevant.

Tip

Documents whose templates have been edited are not always updated when closed and reopened. You may have to restart LibreOffice for the change to take effect.

```
┌─────────────────────────────────────────────────────┐
│ ▌ LibreOffice 4.0.2.2                          _ ▢ ⊠ │
├─────────────────────────────────────────────────────┤
│ ⓘ   The template 'LibreOffice-styles-and-formatting-templates' on which │
│     this document is based, has been modified. Do you want to update    │
│     style based formatting according to the modified template?          │
│     ┌──────────────┐  ┌─────────────┐  ┌─────────────┐                  │
│     │ Update Styles│  │ Keep Old Styles│ │    Help    │                  │
│     └──────────────┘  └─────────────┘  └─────────────┘                  │
└─────────────────────────────────────────────────────┘
```

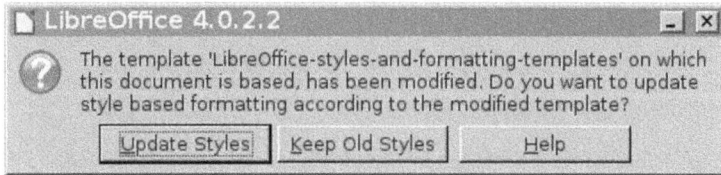

When you open a document, you are warned that its template has been edited.

Generally, you want to avoid detaching documents from their templates. Since the whole point of using templates is to make uniform design easier, the best practices are usually:

- Change the formatting only on the template.

- Always keep documents connected to their templates.

- Never make any formatting changes in a document. Even deleting or adding a style can detach a document from its template.

- As soon as you make changes to the template, close and reopen the documents that use the template as soon as possible. This practice may disturb your work, but it means that you won't have to remember what changed, or wonder if you made an accidental change when you receive notice of the change the next time that you open the file.

Re-attaching styles

Macros and extensions are sometimes available for re-attaching styles to a document. Currently, Template Changer extension is available, but it has not had a release for some time. At any rate, any attempt to swap templates raises the possibility of corruption, so test the extension using duplicate files until you are confident that it works.

A more reliable solution is usually to copy and paste the file contents to a blank file created from the original template.

STOP

Caution

Any changes visible with EDIT > TRACK CHANGES > SHOW CHANGES are lost when you copy and paste.

By contrast, any comments or fields are copied.

Identifying a template

You can always identify a LibreOffice template file, because the second letter in its extension is always a "t." This pattern is used in both Open Document Format and the obsolete OpenOffice.org 1.0 format:

Application	ODF Format	OOo Format
Writer	.ott	.stw
Calc	.ots	.stc
Impress	.otp	.sti
Draw	.otg	.stf

Template extensions for Open Document Format and the older OpenOffice.org format.

Using the Template Manager

LibreOffice does not display template directories directly. Instead, it creates a virtual view of the contents of all the template directories listed in TOOLS > OPTIONS > PATHS > TEMPLATES in the TEMPLATE MANAGER window.

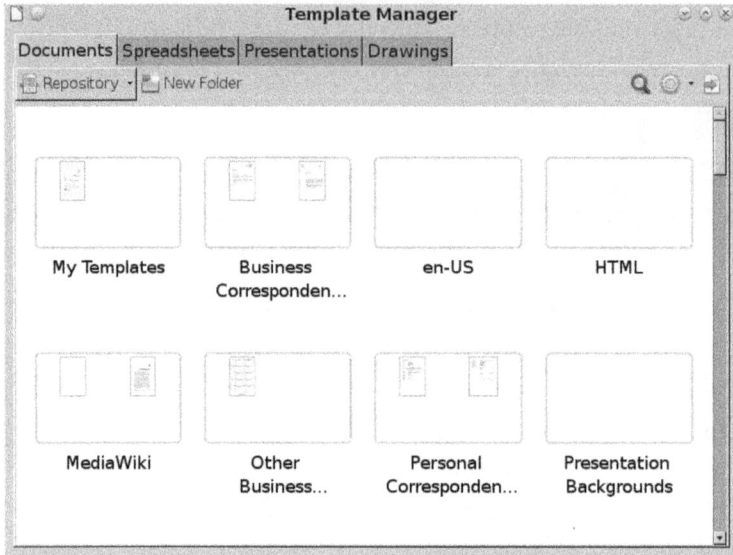

The Template Manager, showing sub-folders for different categories.

The Template Manager opens from several places in the menu. One is FILE > NEW > TEMPLATES. Depending on the version and operating system, it may also open from:

- FILE > SAVE AS TEMPLATE (not available in Apache OpenOffice or some operating systems).

- The TEMPLATES link on the introductory splash screen.
- FILE > TEMPLATES > MANAGE or FILE > TEMPLATEMENU, depending on the operating system and version.

STOP

Caution

Each view of the Template Manager shows only the icons that apply to whatever is selected. For example, in

Linux when you save from TEMPLATEMENU, you can only save, search, and view.

The Template Manager is divided into tabs for different types of templates: DOCUMENTS, SPREADSHEETS, PRESENTATIONS, and DRAWINGS. Within each tab, sub-folders of the templates are shown as rectangles, and referred to as "categories."

As shown above, you might have sub-folders such as EN-US and EN-CA for templates that use American and Canadian English locales for dictionaries.

Other options might be sub-folders named for a client or project or specific themes, such as light or dark backgrounds – whatever works best for you. Click on these rectangles to zoom in on the available templates and select from them.

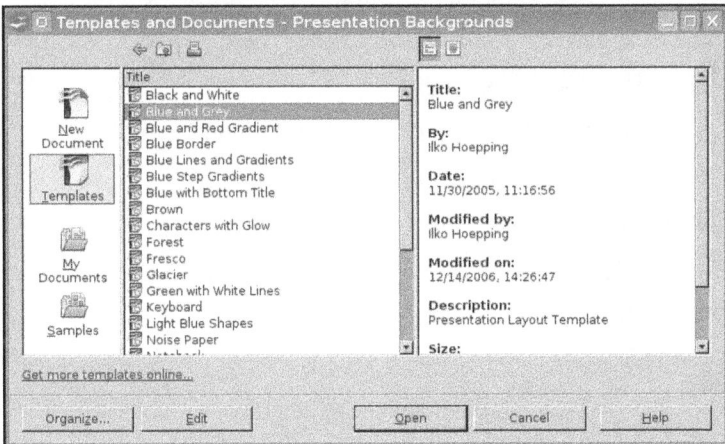

OpenOffice's Template Manager and versions of LibreOffice before 3.3 have an older design that is functionally equivalent.

Planning a template library

Whether you create or download your templates, start by assessing the types of documents you create regularly. Although you might be tempted to download or design every template available, installing or designing more templates than you generally need will only make finding the ones you actually use harder.

Begin your planning by considering what your general layout will be. If you work for a company, does it have corporate colors that you will constantly use? If so, begin by creating the colors in TOOLS > OPTIONS > COLORS so they are available for uses such as table borders and headings in color documents.

Are particular fonts part of your personal or corporate branding? Do you prefer a particular font size? All such items can go into an all-purpose template that can be the starting point for others. Call the result something like GENERAL or STANDARD.

Become more specific by recalling what documents you have written in the past. If you can't remember them:

- Open FILE > RECENT DOCUMENTS.

- Check the attachments in emails that you have sent.

- Keep a diary of the documents you produce over a week or a month and how often you write the same kind.

A carefully selected template can last you for years, so taking the time to classify your work is worth the effort.

Example: Assessing template requirements

Imagine that you are a financial account executive. You want your all-purpose template to use your company's branding.

After some consideration, you find that you are regularly writing one-page memos, short official letters, and longer monthly internal reports. You also write quarterly reports for the company newsletter, whose editor wants copy in HTML, and the occasional personal letter, whose design should make clear that you are not speaking officially for the company.

Basically, in planning your template library, you are answering the question: What documents do I regularly produce in LibreOffice?

If you are like most people, you will probably come up with at least three or four different templates that you will need regularly. If you don't download them, create them gradually as the need arises. Unless some of your templates are extremely similar, you probably won't want to design more than one at a time.

Naming templates

Like style names, template names should be as descriptive as possible. Descriptive titles are simply easier to find in a menu.

However, another practical reason for choosing template names carefully is that, if you copy a file to another computer, you might have a naming conflict. If that happens, your document will not be seen how you meant it to be seen. If you forgot to make a copy, you could have a lot of re-formatting to do.

To avoid such problems, make your template names as specific as possible. For instance, instead of LETTER.OTT, call your template PERSONAL-LETTER – or, better yet, something long and exact like PERSONAL-LETTER-FORMAL-STRUCTURE. The more specific the template's name, the easier it will be to find when you want it.

Readying templates for use

Once you have figured which templates you need, you can get the templates you need in several ways:

- Downloading and installing templates made by others, perhaps with minor modifications.

- Creating your own templates using LibreOffice's wizards as a guide.

- Designing your own templates from scratch.

Regardless of how you obtain templates, they must be registered before LibreOffice can take full advantage of them. See "Saving and registering templates," page 55.

Downloading templates

If you prefer not to design your templates from scratch, you can use pre-existing templates instead, modifying them as necessary.

Almost all the templates that you find online are released under free licenses, so you can generally modify them freely.

The disadvantage of using others' templates is that you have to sort through them to find what you want. At times, you may download two templates from different websites, only to discover that they are the same template with different names.

Often, too, you have to modify downloaded templates to get the exact design you want. In the end, you may not save time so much as exchange the time spent designing for searching and tweaking templates.

Another problem with these official sites is that each template must be downloaded and installed separately.

However, you can find extensions like the Professional Template Pack II that will install multiple templates together from TOOLS > EXTENSION MANAGER after you download them. Using such extensions can save several hours of effort.

You can also open Microsoft Office templates and convert them to Open Document Format. This is an ideal solution for presentation backgrounds, but less so for word processor documents, especially those with complex formatting, which may not import or export well.

STOP

Caution

Using Microsoft Office templates is illegal if you do not have a copy of Microsoft Office. To avoid any legal difficulties – however remote – avoid using templates designed for Microsoft Office except for personal, non-commercial use.

Creating templates with wizards

If designing your own templates is too large a step, start by using the wizards that LibreOffice installs.

These wizards illustrate the kinds of decisions that you make when designing, and can give you a sense of the sorts of decisions you need to make when designing your own templates.

In addition, they are good examples of how to add structure to templates. However, despite their best efforts to provide variety, the wizards do tend to create unimaginative, outdated results.

Wizards are available from the FILE > WIZARDS sub-menu. Some of the wizards give you the option of using a LibreOffice Base database or the address book of an email client for filling in fields, which is convenient for mass mail-outs.

When you are finished setting options for the template, the wizard defaults to saving the resulting template to a subdirectory of your personal template directory, registering them for immediate use.

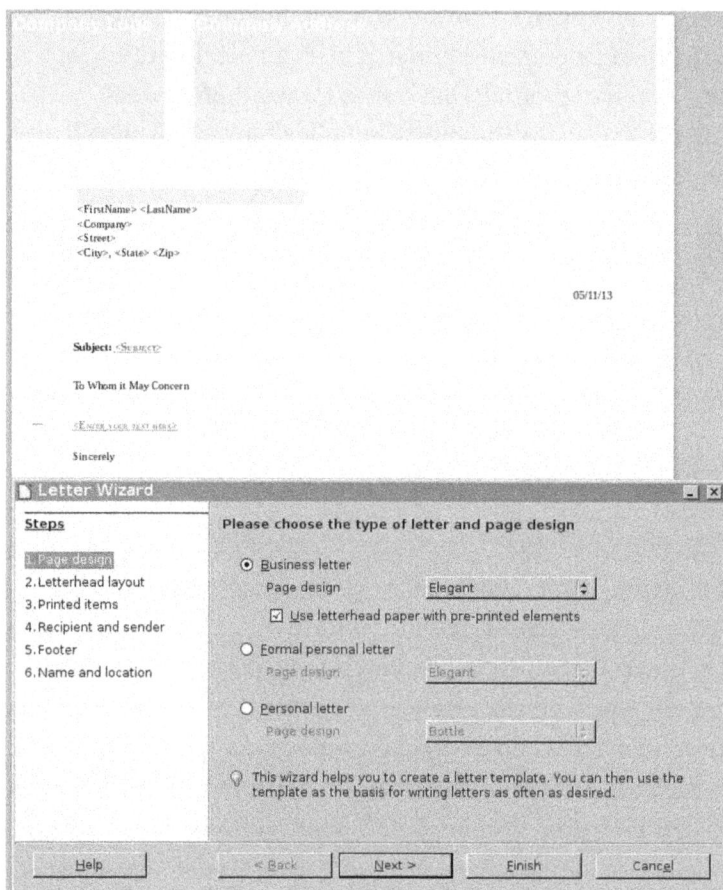

LibreOffice's letter template wizard. Although often more elaborate than strictly necessary, these wizards can give you a starting point to studying templates.

The PRESENTATION template is particularly useful. It is designed as a wizard to guide you through the basic formatting and structural decisions for building a slide show.

Once, Impress opened in its template wizard. It remains a useful reminder of the structural decisions you need to make.

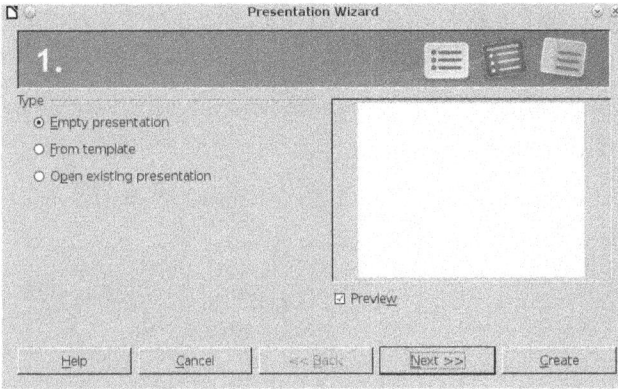

The Presentation Wizard in Impress.

Saving and registering templates

A regular file only needs to be saved in order to be ready for use. By contrast, each template must be registered with LibreOffice before you can use it, just as databases and address books must be.

What this means is that you cannot simply save a template.

True, if you save a file using FILE> SAVE or FILE > SAVE AS, you can select a LibreOffice template from the drop-down list of formats in the SAVE dialog window. This approach is useful for such purposes as saving a template so you can install it on another computer, or give a copy to a friend.

However, a conventional SAVE does not register and activate the new template for use on your system. To make a template available, follow these steps:

1 Save it with FILE > SAVE AS TEMPLATE, FILE > TEMPLATES > SAVE AS TEMPLATE, or FILE > TEMPLATEMENU > SAVE AS TEMPLATE (all

these options may not be available in all versions of LibreOffice).

In each case, the TEMPLATE MANAGER opens, offering a virtual depiction of the templates saved for all users on the system and for your personal use only. The rectangles are sub-folders of the main directories listed in the paths.

You can either click down through the window or use the icons in the upper right to search and sort by name.

If you have recently made several templates, you might need to click REFRESH to have all existing templates display.

2   Click a sub-folder in the display if you want to specify where the template displays in the Template Manager.

STOP Caution

If you do not select a sub-folder, the template is saved to the appropriate tab for its file format, rather than to a sub-folder.

3   Click the SAVE icon at the top left, and give the new template a name. If necessary, you can overwrite an existing template.

The newly saved template is now available for use.

Saving multiple templates

If you have downloaded a large number of templates, you can register a large number of them by moving them to one of the directories listed in the PATHS section of TOOLS > OPTIONS. Alternatively, select from the template manager tool bar REPOSITORY > LOCAL or REPOSITORY > NEW REPOSITORY.

Setting a new default

The default template for each module in LibreOffice is based on several assumptions. It assumes that most users want a generic font, like Times New Roman or Liberation Serif. It assumes that a connection exists between language locale and paper size, so that an installation that defaults to American English will use letter-sized paper, while one that defaults to United Kingdom English will use A4 paper.

These are reasonable assumptions. However, if they don't serve your needs, you can avoid making changes to every generic document that you start by changing the default template.

To change the default template:

1 Create and register the replacement template.

2 Open the Template Manager. Select the replacement default template.

3 Click the SET AS DEFAULT button.

Now, each new document will use the default template unless you specifically choose another template. LibreOffice reverts to its original DEFAULT template (the default DEFAULT) if you delete the replacement default.

Storing template structure

Discussions of templates usually emphasize storing formats in them. However, templates can store everything from return addresses to standard boilerplate such as corporate backgrounders – any information that you re-use but do not care to reinvent or type again. Instead, you can begin writing similar documents either immediately or with only minor modifications.

Such information is especially easy to store in Impress, in which each piece of information can be placed on one slide and easily deleted or rearranged.

Using placeholders

Placeholders are fields that mark the type of information needed at a certain spot, but leave you to fill in the details by clicking them.

Impress has built-in placeholders for slide titles, body text, and inserted objects.

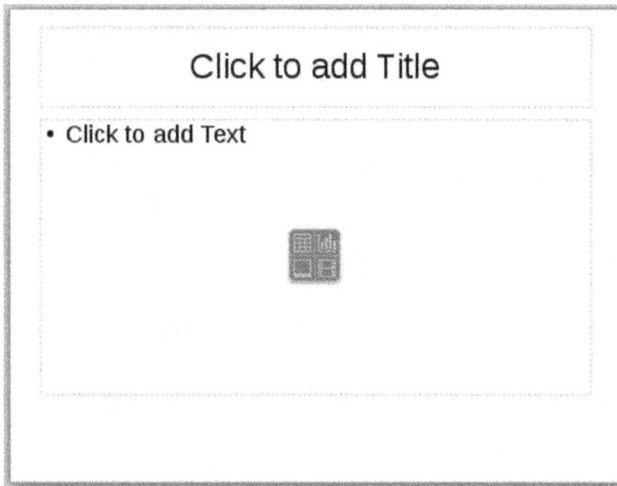

An Impress slide, with placeholders for the title and text, and a generic placeholder for tables, charts, images, and movies in the middle.

Placeholders are fields that mark the type of information needed at a certain spot, but leave you to fill in the details by clicking them.

Impress has built-in placeholders for slide titles, body text, and inserted objects.

However, you can also use placeholders for text and objects in Writer from INSERT > FIELDS > OTHER > FUNCTIONS. Select FORMAT, then give the placeholder a name in the PLACEHOLDER field. The REFERENCE field can be ignored.

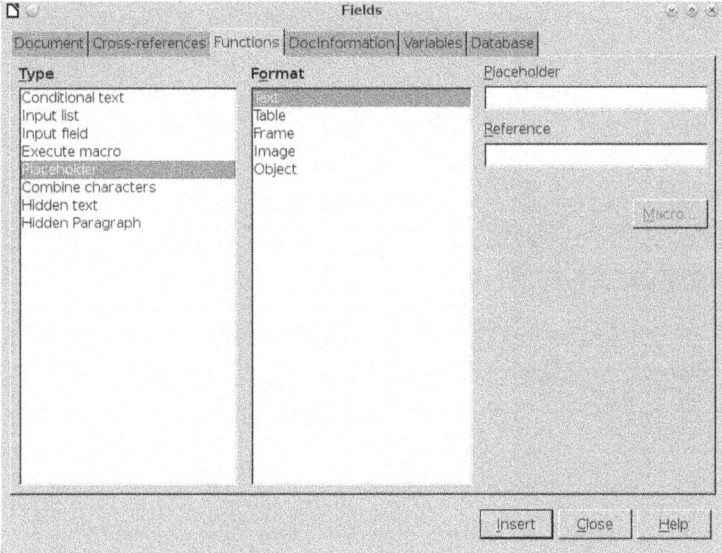

The FIELDS dialog window for adding placeholders in Writer.

The placeholders are added as fields in the document. When you are ready to insert the information, click the placeholder field to replace it.

<SALUTATION> <TITLE> <LAST NAME>

PLACEHOLDER fields in Writer for the opening of a letter.

Tip

Placeholders have their own character style, which makes them easy to find using EDIT > FIND & REPLACE.

Using fields in templates

Fields are another way to store information in templates. Four kinds of fields are likely to be useful:

- System information, such as date and time.

- General user information, stored in TOOLS > OPTIONS > LIBREOFFICE > USER DATA.

- Document information, stored or displayed in FILE > PROPERTIES.

- Document statistics, generated as you create the document. They include page numbers, page counts, and other information commonly placed in the header or footer.

As this information changes, the fields in the template will also change, updating each time that you open the document without you having to change it manually.

Tip

Date and time fields are of two kinds. Fixed fields add the current information and never change. By contrast, variable fields always update to the current date and time when anyone opens a document or update the fields.

Both have uses. For example, you could place a fixed date field beside a witness' signature, and a variable date field at the top of a letter template.

Date and time fields also support a number of formats, defaulting to the one listed for the current language. LibreOffice offers no way to change the default formats permanently.

Although a Month-Day-Year format is common in the United States, increasingly international use favors a consistent sequence – either Year-Month-Day or, less frequently, a Day-Month-Year format. All these formats can have two or four digits for the year.

Example: Using placeholders & fields

LibreOffice includes a tool for designing do-it-yourself business cards. The tool is designed so that you add information on one sample card, then add the information automatically to the rest.

To create the sample card:

1   Go to FILE > BUSINESS CARDS, and select the label sheet to use. Click the NEW DOCUMENT button to continue.

2   Adjust the zoom so you can work comfortably on the sample card.

3   Create two frames of equal width and height from INSERT > FRAME. One is for a graphic on the left, and the other for text on the right.

4   Place the cursor in the left hand frame and select INSERT > FIELDS > OTHER > FUNCTIONS > PLACEHOLDER.

5   Create an Image placeholder and call it GRAPHIC. Click the INSERT button to continue. You do not have to close the FIELDS dialog window to continue.

6   Place the cursor in the right hand frame and create one placeholder per line for AUTHOR, POSITION, COMPANY, EMAIL, and PHONE.

The AUTHOR field is filled automatically with the name entered in the User Data for LibreOffice's general use.

7 Give each line a right alignment. You can further adjust the look of the placeholders by editing the PLACEHOLDER character style.

8 Save the document. The BUSINESS CARD template is now ready for any user to complete by clicking on each placeholder and replacing it with actual information.

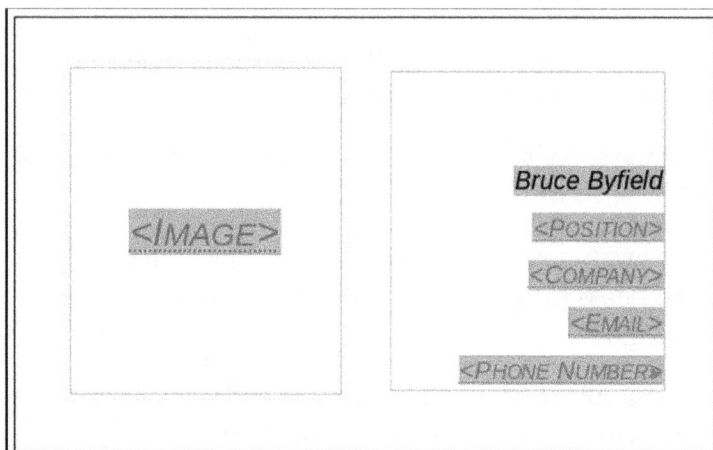

A basic business card template. Placeholders are used for information, and the name is filled in using the AUTHOR field, which borrows information from TOOLS > OPTIONS > LIBREOFFICE > USER DATA > FIRST / LAST NAME.

Editing templates

Unless you are extremely well-organized or lucky, you won't make a perfect template in one sitting. Instead, the first few times you use a template, you are likely to find countless ways to improve it so that it meets your needs without requiring endless manual adjustments.

To open a template for editing, select FILE > TEMPLATES > MANAGE to open the Template Manager, select a template, and click EDIT on the tool bar above the templates.

Once a template is open, you can edit it exactly the same as any other document. However, remember to register your changes by saving with FILE > TEMPLATES > SAVE AS TEMPLATE.

Deleting templates

You can delete custom or imported templates. You cannot delete templates installed with LibreOffice, through an extension, or for the entire system, although you can delete the extension from TOOLS > EXTENSION MANAGER.

From within the Template Manager, select the template to delete, then click the DELETE button.

STOP
Caution

The Template Manager does not include confirmation dialogs. A selected file is deleted as soon as you click the DELETE button. Nor can the deletion be undone.

Exporting templates

You can export a template from the Template Manager. Select the template to export, then click the EXPORT button. Exporting a template takes a copy of the template, de-registers the copy, and saves it to the directory of your choice.

Changing templates

Except with Template Changer or another extension, you cannot directly change which template is used by a document. Nor is there any means to apply multiple templates to the same document. However, you can use three workarounds.

The first is to open a document based on another template, then copy and paste into it. This method works best when all styles in both documents have the same names, because the styles in the original document will take on the formatting of the new document.

Tip

If you experience some problems with graphics, try copying and pasting a few pages at a time instead of all at once.

In addition, any custom-named styles in use in the original document are copied over to the new document. By contrast, custom-named styles that are defined but not in use, as well as tracked changes, will not appear in the new document.

A second method is to create a new master document with a different template. If you import the template-less document into the master document, it will be reformatted while being used from within the master document. When not opened from the master document, it will revert to its original formatting.

The third and most practical method is to transfer styles between documents.

Transferring styles is convenient when two people have been working on a document, but made their own changes to the template (something that happens, although you shouldn't encourage it).

You might also use the feature to transfer manual formatting of a document to its template, although making changes to the template is generally a more reliable practice.

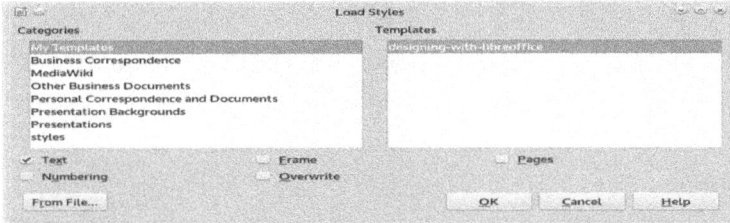

Transferring styles between documents. PARAGRAPH and CHARACTER styles are listed together under TEXT. Click OVERWRITE to replace existing styles of the same name.

To transfer styles between documents:

1   Press F11 to open the Styles and Formatting window.

2   From the pull-down menu at the far right of the icon bar, click LOAD STYLES.

The Load Styles window opens. The CATEGORIES pane shows the sub-folders in the Template Manager, while the template pane shows the templates of the current sub-folder.

3   Either select one of the templates in the Template pane or click the FROM FILE button and select a document template using the file manager.

4   Select the types of styles to import by selecting the boxes along the bottom of the LOAD STYLES window.

Tip

The LOAD STYLES window uses TEXT to refer to both PARAGRAPH and CHARACTER styles.

5   If you want to replace any styles in the current document that have the same name as the ones in the template or document from which you are importing styles, click the OVERWRITE button.

STOP

Caution

Carefully check styles that were supposed to be overwritten. They may not be consistently overwritten if you have large documents and a computer with limited memory.

If you do not want to replace styles, leave the OVERWRITE box unselected. You will import only styles that have names not found in the current document.

6   Click the OK button on the top right. You receive no confirmation, but the importing is complete in a matter of seconds.

Tip

Transferring styles does not change the template listed in FILE > PROPERTIES > GENERAL. If you are unsure whether a document is still associated with a template, make a minor change in the template and see if the document updates the next time that you open LibreOffice.

Working with templates in a file manager

LibreOffice includes all the features you need to interact with templates. Sometimes, however, you may want to deal with templates from outside LibreOffice, either because LibreOffice is not open or because you are dealing with more than one template at a time. Or perhaps you want to organize your installation by adding sub-folders to the main template directories.

In these cases, you can interact with templates through a file manager. The storage directory for templates varies with the operating system and software release, but you can find which directories your installation is using by going to TOOLS > OPTIONS > PATHS > TEMPLATES.

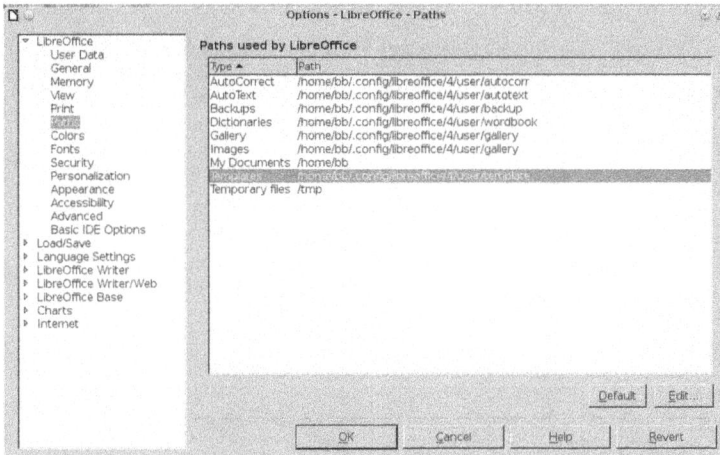

The directory (or directories) where templates are stored is listed in TOOLS > OPTIONS > LIBREOFFICE > PATHS. The exact path differs with operating systems and LibreOffice releases.

You can add directories to the template path, separating them from each other with a semi-colon. If you want to make directories accessible to all users on the system, log in as root or administrator and go to the directory in which LibreOffice was installed. For example, if you downloaded a Linux version directly from The Document Foundation, this directory will be in something like /opt/libreoffice4.4/share/template. In other cases, the top two directories may be different, but the bottom two should be the same.

If you are installing a large number of templates, placing them all in one directory, adding to the path, and re-starting LibreOffice is the quickest way of registering them.

The complete basics

If you have read Chapter 2, you should now have a general sense of how styles and templates work. Neither is difficult in theory, although some of the ways that templates work may seem needlessly complicated until you realize that they exist to prevent file corruption.

In the next chapter, you will learn how styles can automate your work.

4

Styled features and long documents

While you are designing, styles constantly prove their worth. However, styles don't stop giving you advantages when the template is finished. In Writer, paragraph styles also make advanced features more efficient, especially in academic and formal documents.

Tasks such as outlining, navigating documents, adding cross-references, or creating tables of contents are possible without the use of paragraph styles. However, without styles, such features are so much more laborious that doing them manually is a waste of time, except in a few cases where they are unavoidable.

This chapter begins with Writer's advanced features, focusing on both how paragraph styles enhance them, and how you can use them to customize your documents and give them a professional touch. You might say that the chapter is mostly about the unexpected dividends that taking the time to use styles can pay you.

The rest is about the tools for designing long and academic documents. Some of these tools do not rely heavily on styles (if at all), but you may need to be aware of their quirks as you design.

Using outline levels

If you have noticed TOOLS > OUTLINE NUMBERING, you may have assumed that it is a manual method of creating outlines.

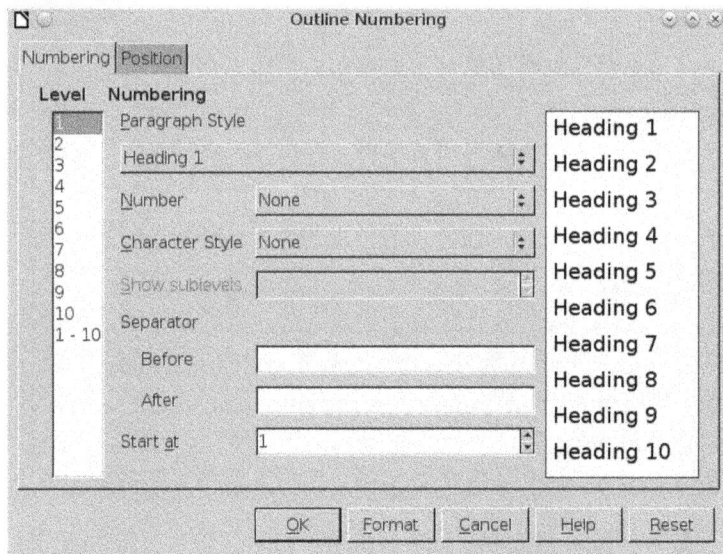

The OUTLINE NUMBERING dialog window is used for more than just formatting outlines.

However, outlines are only the most basic use of outline numbering. More importantly, outline numbering also defines the paragraph styles used for each level. These styles are picked up by other Writer tools to simplify your work.

By default, each outline level is assigned a heading paragraph style, with HEADING 1 assigned to outline LEVEL 1, and so on with each heading style corresponding to the same outline level.

Styles and Templates

However, what most users never notice is that you can assign any other paragraph style to any outline level, by using the OUTLINE LEVEL field on the OUTLINE & NUMBERING tab for a paragraph style. You can also change the default style for an outline level by editing the PARAGRAPH STYLE field in TOOLS > OUTLINE NUMBERING.

Once a paragraph style is assigned to an outline level, it can be used for:

- Writing an outline.

- Outlining in the Navigator.

- Setting up cross-references in the most efficient manner.

- Creating tables of contents and formatting indexes and bibliographies.

Writing an outline

You can outline using heading paragraph styles with a list style attached to them, or a single paragraph style with an outline list style attached.

However, the most obvious method is to use TOOLS > OUTLINE NUMBERING. The settings for this tool resemble the choices on the OPTIONS tab of a list style. The formatting can be customized separately for each outline level, or for all levels at once.

Outlining in the Navigator

The Navigator is one of the most under-used features of LibreOffice. However, the longer the document, the more useful it becomes as you edit and revise

To open the Navigator, select VIEW > NAVIGATOR, or press the F5 key, or select the Navigator in the sidebar.

On the simplest level, the Navigator lists all of a document's objects, including outline levels – headings by default, other paragraph styles as well if you edit outline levels. Clicking a list item in the Navigator jumps to it in the editing window.

However, what may be less apparent is that the headings listed in the Navigator can help to restructure a document.

Tip

Tables, frames, and other objects are most useful for navigation if you give them descriptive names rather than accepting defaults like TABLE6 or IMAGE12. One choice is to give all pictures the same name as their original files. That way, finding the files becomes easier.

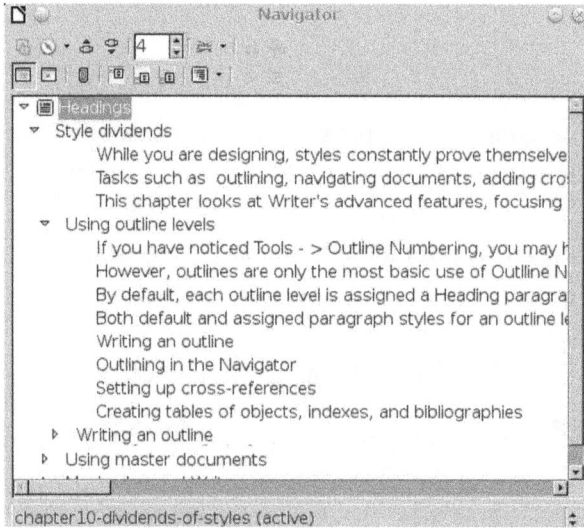

The Navigator becomes a more powerful outlining tool if you set an Outline Level to show the TEXT BODY paragraph style.

Changing outline levels using the Navigator

Headings should be hierarchical, so that the topic in a HEADING 3 paragraph style is contained by the HEADING 2 paragraph style directly above it. For example, the heading "The Human Body" might have sub-headings below it of "The Heart" and "The Lungs." This structuring strengthens the internal logic of a document, and helps readers find sections when they scan.

Such relationships are essential to the structure of a document. If you see a heading that should be raised or lowered in the hierarchy, highlight it and then click either PROMOTE LEVEL or DEMOTE LEVEL, the buttons on the bottom right of the tool bar.

Each time you click, the currently selected heading will be raised or lowered one level in the hierarchy. So will any outline levels subordinate to it, so that promoting a HEADING 2 outline level to HEADING 1 also promotes all HEADING 3 outline levels between it and the next HEADING 2.

Moving material using the Navigator

Similarly, as you work, you may find that part of the contents belongs somewhere else in the document.

Instead of cutting and pasting, you can click either PROMOTE CHAPTER or DEMOTE CHAPTER, the buttons on the top right of the tool bar, to move a heading and the text beneath it to a new place in the document.

Tip

In the Navigator, "chapter" refers to the part of the document between one heading and the next. "Promoting" moves the chapter closer to the start of the document, "demoting" moves it closer to the end.

All subordinate headings and any other paragraph styles underneath the selected heading will also move, keeping the same position in relation to each other, but changing their group position in the document.

In effect, the Navigator replaces ordinary copying and pasting. However, it is more effective than copying and pasting, because it provides a visual image of your actions.

Just as importantly, if you are interrupted, with the Navigator there is no danger of losing content because you have forgotten about it.

Using cross-references

Cross-references are updatable fields that refer to another part of a document. In online documents, they are links for easy navigation to the reference.

Manual cross-references would be difficult to maintain – especially their page references—so LibreOffice keeps them automatically updated as you add and delete material and close and open documents. You can also manually update by clicking TOOLS > UPDATE > FIELDS.

To add a cross-reference, you need two elements: the SELECTION or source, and the REFERENCE or target. The SELECTIONS are chosen either from the contents of outline levels or from bookmarks or markers added manually.

Usually, you should add cross-references as your document is being finished. That way, you avoid breaking links and having to re-create them as you move passages around or rename files. Also, you can keep the cross-reference dialog window open and do all cross-references in one effort.

If you plan to use cross-references for tables, images, and other elements, give each element a caption, then assign the CAPTION paragraph style to an outline level.

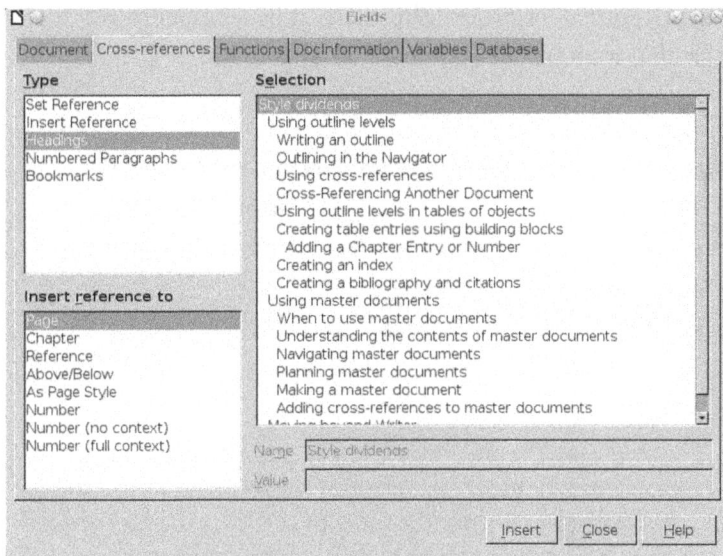

Outline levels simplify adding cross-references. The alternative is to set references, either manually or as bookmarks.

Cross-referencing within one document

Outline levels provide automatic markers to use with cross-references. Add headings as you write, then follow these steps when you add cross-references:

1 Place the cursor in the position for the first cross-reference.

2 Select INSERT > CROSS REFERENCE. The FIELDS dialog window opens on the CROSS-REFERENCES tab.

3   From the TYPE pane, select the sort of source to use. Use HEADINGS whenever possible, since you are adding them anyway and they tend to be relatively short. Otherwise, consider NUMBERED PARAGRAPHS or BOOKMARKS.

    When all else fails, you can use SET REFERENCE to manually create a source. However, this method is so cumbersome and slow that it should be avoided if at all possible.

4   Choose the source from the SELECTION pane.

5   Choose the format for the reference from the INSERT REFERENCE TO pane. Click the INSERT button to insert the cross-reference into your document. The FIELDS dialog window remains open.

Tip

ABOVE/BELOW are informal, and should be avoided in academic or legal documents. Avoid using them unless the document is nearly completed, in case you move passages around and change their relationship.

6   In the document, add the words to introduce the cross-reference. For instance, if the structure you are using includes the chapter and page number, the cross-reference dialog inserts only the actual chapter and page number.

    The complete reference may require something like, "See Chapter 6, page 79." Alternatively, you might want to mention the heading.

Tip

You can add the wording around the text as AutoText. For instance, you could have one AutoText entry or Custom field for "See Chapter " and another for ", page " (notice the spaces at the end of both).

Repeat for all the other cross-references. Close the dialog window when done.

Tip

Cross-references work differently in master documents. See "Adding cross-references between sub-documents," page 105.

Cross-referencing to another file

Adding a cross-reference to another document is a different process from adding a cross-reference within a single document, even if both the source and the target document are in the same master document.

The two basic methods involve using SET REFERENCE or hyperlinking using styles. Both methods are done manually.

Using styles saves time when you are cross-referencing another file. In fact, using SET REFERENCE to create a manual reference is sufficiently confusing that I recommend avoiding it altogether.

To add a hyperlink using styles, follow this procedure:

1 Open the target document for the cross-reference. The target document is the one which contains the cross-reference.

2　Open the Navigator by selecting VIEW > NAVIGATOR, or pressing the F5 key, or selecting it in the sidebar.

3　Select the source document (the document which you are referencing) from the drop-down list at the bottom of the Navigator.

4　Set the DRAG MODE tool to INSERT AS HYPERLINK.

5　Drag the heading you are referencing into the target document.

A hyperlink to the heading is placed in the target document. The hyperlink is active and can be used online to jump to the source document.

Tip

If you want the hyperlink to resemble regular text, edit the INTERNET LINK and VISITED INTERNET LINK character styles to remove the colors and underlining. This change will affect all hyperlinks, not just cross-references.

6　If necessary, add:

- The introductory text. You can define fields or AutoText to avoid having to type it.

- The page number. It must be added and updated manually.

- The document name. Add it manually, or by dragging and dropping the title of the source document.

Using outline levels in tables and indexes

"Indexes and Tables" is the term LibreOffice uses to describe fields that are generated from the contents of a document.

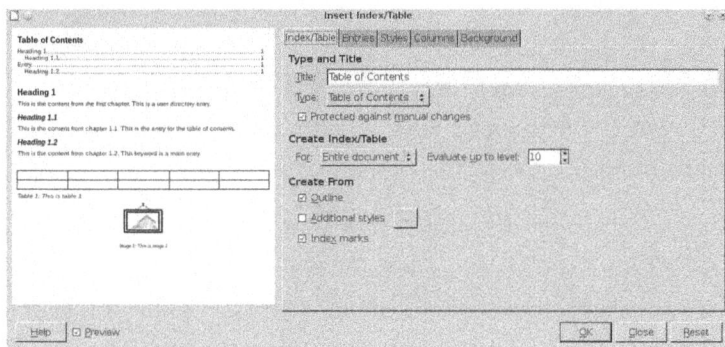

INSERT INDEX/TABLE includes tools for extensive customization of tables of contents and similar tables.

The most common are a table of contents (TOC), which is created from outline levels. and tables of illustrations and tables, which are created from captions.

However, you can create all sorts of indexes and tables, such as:

- Alphabetical Index: A list of keywords and their appearances in the text – in other words, a regular index.

- Table of Illustrations: A list of images, generated from caption categories.

- Table of Tables: A list of tables, generated from caption categories.

- Table of Objects: A list of other elements, such as charts.

- Bibliography: A list of reference materials used in the document.

You can also add user-defined index marks to create other tables.

Creating a table of contents

Each kind of table has its own list of customized features. However, the procedure for building most of them is similar to the one for creating a table of contents:

1 If necessary, customize a page style for the table, and add it to the document.

2 Go to INSERT > INDEXES AND TABLES > INDEXES AND TABLES > INDEX/TABLES > TYPE and select the type of table. Your selection determines both the default title and some of the advanced options. However, many of the advanced options may be unnecessary.

3 Select INDEX/TABLES > ADDITIONAL STYLES to add additional paragraph styles to the table of contents. Any selection you make does not add styles to the outline levels.

Tip

Styles already assigned to outline levels cannot be given different outline levels.

4 If your table entries are single words or phrases of a few words, you might be able to save space by setting 2–4 columns on the COLUMNS tab.

5 On the ENTRIES tab, customize the table entries using the building blocks in the STRUCTURE field.

Tip

Keep the LS (Link Start) at the beginning of the ENTRY field, and the LE (Link End) at the end of the field.

These two links make the entire entry a hyperlink to the text, that you can use in an online document or when editing.

Other fields appear in the tab as you make selections. The preview pane on the left shows what your design will look like on the page.

6 Click the OK button to add the table. You can right-click the table to edit or update it later.

7 Edit the paragraph styles for each table entry. These styles consist of a heading paragraph style (for instance, CONTENTS HEADING for a table of contents), and styles for each outline level of table entry (such as CONTENTS 1-10 for Index/Tables).

Usually, you can model the CONTENTS HEADING paragraph style on the document's HEADING 1 or 2 style, and the entry styles on TEXT BODY, using the INHERIT FROM field on the ORGANIZER tab. There is no need to use different font sizes or colors to distinguish the style for each entry level – the left indent is enough.

An alphabetical index will have an index separator style for the alphabetical delimiters at the start of each section.

Structuring table entries with building blocks

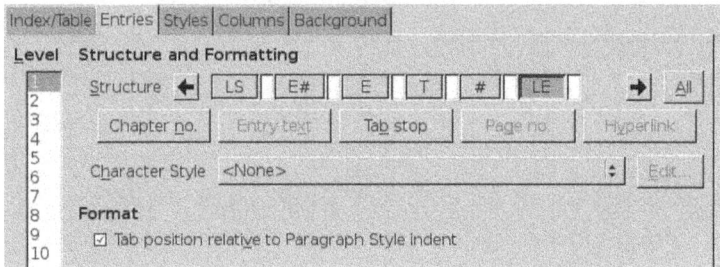

Use building blocks to customize tables of contents.

Unlike most word processors, LibreOffice provides the tools for customizing each entry for a TOC or similar table. These tools are located at INSERT > INDEXES AND TABLES > INDEXES AND TABLES > ENTRIES. You can also modify indexes and tables by customizing their paragraph styles.

The tools consist of a STRUCTURE field in which you can arrange building blocks such as PAGE NUMBER and CHAPTER NUMBER, characters, and spaces to create a standard entry.

Below the field are the unused building blocks. When you add a block to the field, it may become grayed out and unselectable.

Similarly, when you delete a block from the field, it reappears in the unused list below the STRUCTURE field.

When a building block is selected, it looks sunken in the STRUCTURE field. In addition, formatting choices for the building block appear in the window.

Each outline level can be customized separately, or together by pressing the ALL button on the right side of the window. If the levels have common elements, format them together, then edit each level separately for unique features.

As you design, remember:

- Use the LS (Link Start) at the beginning of the ENTRY field and the LE (Link End) at the end of the field to make the entire entry a hyperlink.

- The spacing of all tabs is added to the BEFORE TEXT indentation on the INDENTS AND SPACING tab for each entry's paragraph style (CONTENTS 1-10). To avoid difficulties, leave the BEFORE TEXT field set to o.

- You can reliably use only one tab in the ENTRY field. Otherwise, spacing can become erratic.

- You can add manual spaces and text as well as building blocks to an entry. Manual spaces are inelegant, but can sometimes be a workaround to the one-tab limit.

Avoiding the default TOC design

Table of Contents

The standard word-processor design for a Table of Contents. Its need for crutch-like leader dots between the text entry and the page number is enough to prove it a crippled design.

TOCs in LibreOffice default to a format that has become standard in many word processors. In this style, each entry consists of text and a page number placed by a tab on the right margin. In between are fill characters, usually a period.

If you have regularly generated TOCs using word processors, you might not see anything wrong with the default TOC designs in Writer. Probably, you have seen the design too many times to be bothered by it.

However, to anyone with design knowledge, the result is a failed design. Starting the TOC entry at the left margin and placing the page number against the right margin disassociates them, and the leader dots are needed to try to reconnect them.

The result is ugly. It is also clumsy. Since periods are used to indicate a stop, not a continuation, the periods do not lead the eye across the page. A design that does not disassociate the text entries and the page number in the first place is far more efficient, and simpler as well.

Fortunately, while LibreOffice defaults to this design, you can work with the building blocks and paragraph styles to create a more functional design in any number of ways. For instance:

- Reduce the space between the entry text and the page number using the paragraph style.

Table of Contents

Style dividends 1
   Using outline levels 3
      Writing an outline 4
   How-to: Cross-references with outline
   levels 10

Larger fonts and no leader dots improves the design. But watch for entries that spill over on to another line, spoiling the symmetry of the design for no reason.

- Select the # (Page no.) block and give its character style a larger font size and/or a color to make it stand out more. The

Styles and Templates

larger page number helps to keep the association between the text entries and page numbers.

Table of Contents

Increasing the size of the page number helps some, but the basic problem remains: The distance from some page entries still makes the table of contents harder to read than necessary.

- Click on the T (Tab) block. Fields for the fill character and tab stop position appear below the list of unused building blocks. Replace the fill character with an underscore, and at least your eye is guided continuously across the page, which is an improvement on leader dots. However, having a fill character at all still seems like a needless addition.

Table of Contents

An underscore leads the eye across the page, but still tends to separate the text entries from the page numbers.

- Go to INSERT > INDEXES AND TABLES > INDEXES AND TABLES > COLUMNS and set the table to use two columns. This solution shortens the distance between the text entry and the page number, but may be impractical if any entry text is more than a few words long and spills over onto another line.

Table of Contents

A two-column table of contents lessens the space between text entries and page numbers. However, to work without the problem of long entries taking up two lines, it requires short text entries, or perhaps a landscape oriented page with columns.

- Delete the TAB block and manually add spaces between the E (Entry text) and # (Page no.) blocks. Manual spaces are generally not a good way of laying out design elements, but in this one case, they do not create any problem beyond the need to keep count. They are inelegant, but work.

Table of Contents

A ragged right table of contents keeps text entries and page numbers together so that they can be easily read. However, two ragged margins looks cluttered.

One way to avoid ragged right looking cluttered is to format the Contents paragraph styles so that all entries have the same margin on the left. However, this solution hides the hierarchal structure of the headings.

- Reverse the order of the text entries and the page numbers, with a tab or a couple of manual spaces between them.

Table of Contents

Placing the page numbers before the text entries keep their relation clear and gives the most space for long text entries.

Tip

You can also add a special character or dingbat between the text and page number.

Adding a chapter number

In Writer, you can add chapter numbers to page numbers in the body of a document. However, although the building blocks on the ENTRY tab include a chapter number, your ability to add chapter numbers in a table of contents is limited.

The chapter number building block can only be used in the top level entry in the table of contents. The building block draws its information from the top outline level (usually, the HEADING 1 paragraph style) if the outline level or the paragraph style includes numbering. In the same circumstances in a master document, each top outline level continues the numbering from the previous heading at the same outline level.

Other outline levels cannot display the chapter number, even if you add the building block to its structure on the ENTRIES tab.

Table of Contents

A table of contents that adds the chapter number as a prefix.

As an alternative, ignore the building blocks and attach a list style to the CONTENTS 1 paragraph style. The list style could also be used to add the word "Chapter" before the number.

Creating an index

An index is created in much the same way as a table of objects. The main difference is that it is built from tags of individual words or phrases, rather than from paragraph styles, which would not provide the type of information that an index requires. These tags display in the document as fields.

Adding index entries

The simplest way to add an entry is by selecting words or phrases and marking them with INSERT > INDEXES AND TABLES > INDEX ENTRY. However, it is laborious and time-consuming.

Instead, you can automate the creation of index entries by selecting APPLY TO ALL SIMILAR TEXTS to add other occurrences of an entry in the document. Use MATCH CASE and WHOLE WORDS ONLY to modify the selection of similar texts.

No matter how you prepare them, indexes can have a main entry, and up to two sub-entry levels. Any more sub-entries would generally be overly-complicated for writers to maintain and readers to follow.

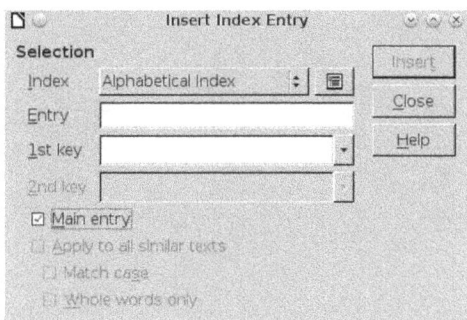

The INSERT INDEX ENTRY dialog window stays open after you insert an entry, letting you move on immediately to the next entry.

Generating an index

After all the entries are created, open the INSERT INDEX/TABLE dialog window to generate the index.

Tip

A standard index is called an ALPHABETICAL INDEX on the TYPE field in the INSERT INDEX/TABLE dialog window. Since this is a non-standard usage, you might modify the title to "Index."

If your entries are short, you can save pages by clicking INSERT > INDEXES AND TABLES > INDEXES AND TABLES > INDEX/TABLES > COLUMNS, and setting the index to use two columns.

If you want to add headings with letters of the alphabet, select INSERT > INDEXES AND TABLES > INDEXES AND TABLES > INDEX/TABLES > ENTRIES > ALPHABETICAL DELIMITER. Alphabetical delimiters are sub-headings, with one for each letter of the alphabet.

Alphabetical Index

A selection from an alphabetical index.

Creating a concordance

A more systematic way to create an index is to use a concordance file. A concordance is a file that lists words to add to the index. It is a plain text file with one word or phrase defined on each line.

Each line has a strict structure, consisting of seven fields, separated by a semi-colon:

SEARCH TERM; ALTERNATIVE ENTRY;1ST KEY;2ND KEY;MATCH CASE; WORD ONLY

No space is entered between the semi-colon and a field's contents. A key is a higher level heading that a search term is placed beneath. For instance, if your search term is "styles," you might want to use the keys "LibreOffice" and "office applications."

If you choose not to have an alternative entry, a first key or a second key, leave the field blank, so that one semi-colon immediately follows another.

The last two fields are structured somewhat differently. If you want only entries that have the same upper or lower case letters as your entries, enter 1 in the second to last field. Similarly, entering 1 in the last field sets the index to only include instances where the entry is a whole word, and not part of a larger one. You can also just leave the last two fields blank, as you can with any of the others.

For example, entering:

MACAW;ARA;PARROTS;;0;0

Would produce an entry for "macaw" with

- A listing under "macaw."

- An alternate listing under "ara" (the scientific name).

- A listing of "Parrots, Macaw."

- No second key (notice the two semi-colons).

- Inclusion of instances that start with a lower or upper case letter (both "macaw" and "Macaw").

- Inclusion of instances in which the term is a whole word or part of a longer word.

Whether creating a concordance is faster than adding entries manually is debatable since the tasks are so different. However, a concordance is certainly more systematic and possibly less tedious.

The disadvantage of a concordance is that it can produce an index that includes instances of common words that are irrelevant for your purposes. In many cases, a useful index may require a combination of manual entries and a concordance.

Creating citations and bibliographies

Like tables of contents and indexes, bibliographies are generated with the INDEX/TABLE dialog window. However, the contents are based upon citations that refer to entries in the TOOLS > BIBLIOGRAPHY DATABASE.

The bibliography database has to cover many different media and circumstances, which is why it contains so many fields. It also includes fields such as ISBN that no citation style uses, but might be useful to you as you do your research.

In practice, however, any single entry in the bibliography needs only about half a dozen fields filled in, no matter what citation format you use. What differs is the fields needed for each type of source material and the order of the fields in each citation style.

However, all citations use the IDENTIFIER field (first on the left) to set the format for a citation in the document. In this column, you can add the citation in the correct form for the citation style.

For example, in the APA style, a citation to this book would use "Byfield" in the text and follow the information cited with (2015).

All necessary information, including the IDENTIFIER field should be entered before any citation is created. In theory, you can add a citation manually by highlighting text, but doing so makes consistency much more difficult.

Tip

Writer has a single bibliography database for all documents. Since formatting entries can be tedious, consider creating a template with citations for each type of source material.

The bibliography database is the source for citations in the text, no matter what citation style you use.

STOP

Caution

Confusingly, the IDENTIFIER column and the SHORT NAME field below the table are the same field, and should have the same content.

To complicate matters even more, the sample entries for both the IDENTIFIER column and the SHORT NAME field are meaningless, although they have been in OpenOffice.org and LibreOffice for over a decade. Replace them with the proper format for the citation style you are using.

Building citations and bibliographies

This procedure is an overview of the steps in creating citations and bibliographies. More detailed information follows:

Bibliography

LibreOffice Documentation Team, *LibreOffice 4.2 Impress Guide.* Friends of Open Document, 2013

LibreOffice Documentation Team, *LibreOffice 4.3 Writer Guide.* Friends of Open Document, 2015

Weber, Jean Hollis, *Self Publishing Using LibreOffice Writer.* Friends of Open Document, 2013

A short bibliography generated by Writer. The book titles use a character style so they appear in italics.

1   Enter the correct information for each source you are using. For example, a reference to a journal article requires different information from a reference to a book.

2   Add the format for citations in the IDENTIFIER column and the SHORT NAME fields.

3   Position the cursor in the text and click INSERT > INDEXES AND TABLES > BIBLIOGRAPHY ENTRY. Use the drop-down list in the SHORT NAME FIELD to chose the citation from the ones you have prepared in the bibliography database, then click the INSERT button. The INSERT BIBLIOGRAPHY ENTRY dialog window remains open, so you can insert citations without having to re-open the dialog for each one.

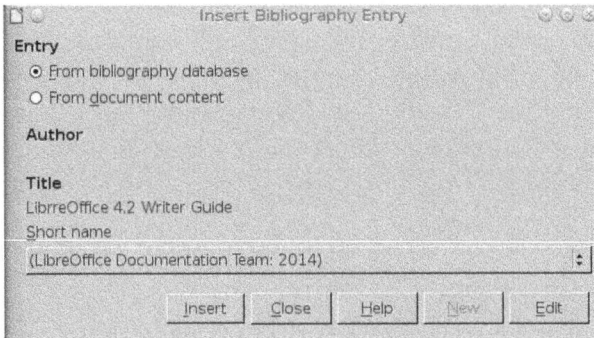

By collecting references in the bibliography database, you can add consistent citations to your document.

4 Place the cursor where you want the bibliography to appear in the text, and select INSERT > INDEXES AND TABLES > INDEXES AND TABLES. Usually, a bibliography appears at the end of a document.

5 Format the bibliography. At a minimum, you will need to:

• Set the TYPE field to BIBLIOGRAPHY on the INDEX/TABLE tab. The TYPE refers to the kind of source, such as a periodical or a web page.

• Use the POSITION field on the ENTRIES tab to structure each type of source used in the document.

• On the ENTRIES tab, set SORT BY. In most modern citation styles, you will want CONTENT (alphabetical descending order), but you can add other sorting criteria, or use ascending alphabetical order.

For example, the default is to arrange a bibliography in the order in which citations appear in the document, rather than alphabetical.

Similarly, the Structure field begins by default with the Short Name for each item, which is not needed.

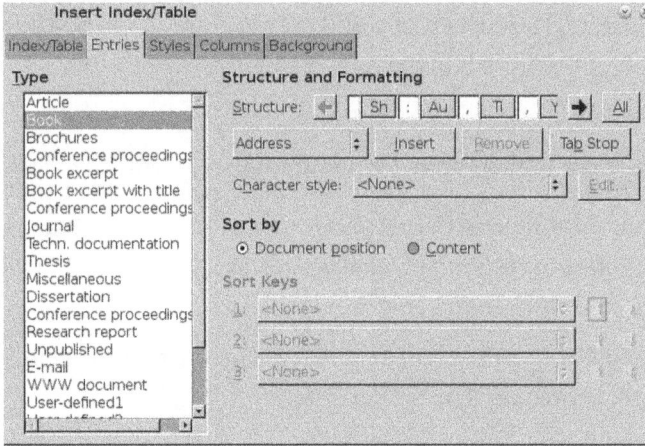

Create a structure for each type of source material used in the document.

6 Adjust the Bibliography paragraph styles. Usually, they will be similar to the Text Body styles.

Preparing bibliographic formats

Before adding citations, you need the correct information for the citation style you are using. Similarly, you need to have the correct information for each bibliography entry.

Most citations styles developed in different fields of academic study. They are a matter of convention, since they all give similar information.

There are five main styles. If you are taking a class or writing for a journal, ask your teacher or editor which format they prefer.

Otherwise, use the format for your field of study:

- APA (American Psychological Association): Psychology, education, and other social sciences.
- MLA (Modern Languages Association): Literature, art, and humanities.
- Chicago: History and specific publications.
- Turabian: A variation of the Chicago style for general use by university students.
- AMA (American Medical Association): Medicine, health, and biology.

Citations within the text require entries in different fields in the bibliography database, and different presentations in the text.

Today, all except the AMA style favor parenthetical citation, in which minimal information is presented in parentheses in the text. Parentheses are less distracting when you read and keep citations from being an exact duplication of the bibliography.

The AMA style uses footnotes or endnotes instead.

The following table shows what fields to use for three common sources: books, articles, and web pages. Fields are arranged from top to bottom in the order that they appear.

STOP Caution

LibreOffice's bibliography database has not been updated for years. Meanwhile, citation styles have changed dramatically, many becoming simpler. For this reason, in case of conflict, use the information and order given here or online in preference to the defaults on the ENTRIES tab.

Format	Book	Journal	Web page
APA	AUTHOR(S)	AUTHOR(S)	AUTHOR(S)
	YEAR	YEAR	YEAR OR [DATE]
	TITLE	TITLE	TITLE
	[CITY]	JOURNAL	Retrieved from:
	PUBLISHER	NUMBER/SERIES	[WEBPAGE]
		PAGE(S)	URL
MLA	AUTHOR(S)	AUTHOR(S)	AUTHOR(S)
	TITLE	TITLE	TITLE
	[CITY]	JOURNAL	PUBLISHER
	PUBLISHER	NUMBER/SERIES	YEAR or [DATE]
	YEAR	YEAR	
		PAGE(S)	
Chicago	AUTHOR(S)	AUTHOR(S)	AUTHOR(S)
	YEAR	YEAR	YEAR
	TITLE	TITLE	TITLE
	[CITY]	JOURNAL	PUBLISHER
	PUBLISHER	NUMBER/SERIES	Accessed: YEAR
		PAGE(S)	or [DATE]
			URL
Turabian	AUTHOR(S)	AUTHOR(S)	AUTHOR(S)
	YEAR	YEAR	YEAR
	TITLE	TITLE	TITLE
	[CITY]	JOURNAL	PUBLISHER
	PUBLISHER	NUMBER/SERIES	Accessed: YEAR
		PAGE(S)	or [DATE]
			URL

AMA			
	AUTHOR(S)	AUTHOR(S)	AUTHOR(S)
	TITLE	TITLE	TITLE
	[CITY]	JOURNAL	PUBLISHER
	PUBLISHER	YEAR	YEAR
	YEAR	NUMBER/VOLUME	Available at: URL
		PAGE[S]	Accessed: YEAR or [DATE]

Preparing citations

Citations in the text need to be prepared beforehand. Edit the IDENTIFIER and SHORT NAME (which are different names for the same field) using the format indicated in the table below. Fields are listed from the top in the order in which they should appear:

Format	Datab.	Citations	Other
APA	YEAR	(YEAR)	Mention the author at the start of the sentence that includes the citation.
MLA	AUTHOR	(AUTHOR pages)	Add title if different sources are used by the same author.
Chicago	AUTHOR YEAR	(AUTHOR, YEAR, pages)	Older version uses footnotes or endnotes.
Turabian	AUTHOR YEAR	(AUTHOR, YEAR, pages)	
AMA	–	Footnote or endnote	Footnote or endnote.

The bibliography database fields need for in-text citations, and the citation formats.

Creating footnotes and endnotes

Parenthetical citations have the advantage of letting you view them without losing your place in the text. However, footnotes and endnotes are still used for citations in the AMA format as well for personal preferences.

To use the bibliography database for footnotes and endnotes, set up the citation in the IDENTIFIER column of the bibliography database. The citation may be much longer than most parenthetical citations, but you can still use the column.

To position a footnote or endnote, click INSERT > FOOTNOTE/ENDNOTE. After the number, complete the footnote or endnote by selecting the citation from the drop-down list for INSERT > INDEXES AND TABLES > BIBLIOGRAPHY ENTRY > SHORT NAME.

Using master documents

Master documents are meta-documents: documents made from a collection of Writer documents. Like many advanced aspects of Writer, they work best with a consistent use of templates and styles.

You view the structure of a master document through a specialized version of the Navigator that you can toggle on and off on the tool bar's left.

A master document contains links to its sub-documents. When sub-documents are opened, they are reformatted according to the master document's template. You can print from a master document, and edit text created in one, but all sub-documents must be opened separately to edit them.

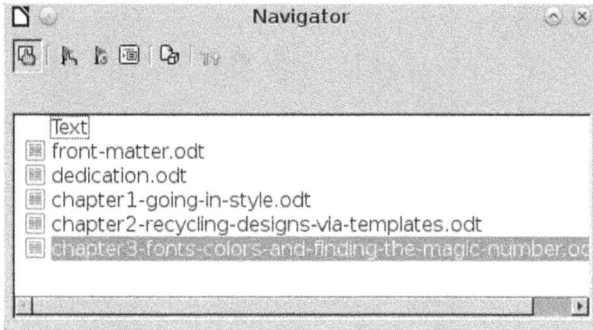

Navigator
Text
front-matter.odt
dedication.odt
chapter1-going-in-style.odt
chapter2-recycling-designs-via-templates.odt
chapter3-fonts-colors-and-finding-the-magic-number.od

The Navigator includes a special view for the contents of master documents.

Tip

The reformatting applies only within the master document. If the sub-documents use their own template, they format differently when opened separately.

When to use master documents

Consider using master documents when:

- Your computer's memory is limited, so you are working with small documents.

- Material is used in different places. A sub-document can be included in more than one master document.

- A document (such as a book) has multiple authors. Authors can work on sub-documents (such as chapters) by themselves, then you use the master document for assembling the complete document.

- You want to produce two or more documents that are similar except in some parts. You can add all the files for all the sub-documents, then hide or unhide individual sections.

Understanding master documents' contents

Master documents are built from three sources:

- Sub-documents: Smaller, individual files. You can edit one by selecting it in the Navigator, and selecting EDIT from the right-click menu. Sub-documents help multiple authors to work on the same master document at the same time.

- Indexes and tables of objects inserted into text areas of the master document. Like any text, they can be replaced by sub-documents.

- Text: Areas between sub-documents that are part of the master document. In Navigator's master document view, each text area is only labeled as TEXT, so their use should be minimized to avoid confusion. You might find the parts of the master document easier to keep track of if you avoid text and use sub-documents instead.

Navigating master documents

Master documents have a special view in the Navigator. To toggle the view, click the TOGGLE button in the upper left of the tool bar. A new set of icons appears in the toolbar.

The Navigator icons for the master document view.

Tip

The Navigator only inserts items above the current one, You can rearrange items after adding them.

Planning master documents

To use master documents efficiently:

- If possible, use the same template to create the master document and all its sub-documents. A sub-document with a different template may have formatting problems when you switch between using it by itself and using it as a sub-document. If you are using a sub-document in more than one master document, ignore this advice and hope for the best.

- Place a master document and all of its sub-documents in the same directory.

- Ordinarily, you probably want each part of a master document to start on a separate page. You can set this format up automatically using the BREAKS section on the TEXT FLOW tab of paragraph styles to start a new page after the paragraph style that begins all the sub-documents, such as HEADING 1..

- The convention is to start each new part of a long document on a right, odd-numbered page. The reason is that most readers' eyes fall on the right page first. If you want a page to be a right page, add a blank text in the master document. Do not uses spaces to add another page, or you may run into difficulties.

- Aside from tables and indexes and page breaks, minimize the content that is added to the master document directly, rather than to sub-documents. The more content that is added directly to the master document, the more likely it is likely to crash.

- Use page styles and/or manual page breaks to use different numbering for different parts of the master document. For example, one common format is use lower case roman numerals for front matter such as copyright pages and tables of contents, and Arabic numbers for the main text. Often, too, numbering is restarted with the main text.

STOP Caution

Currently, master documents can have problems with page breaks. If you have difficulties, assemble long files by copying and pasting.

Creating master documents

Master documents can be fragile to work with. Creating one in this order should minimize problems:

1 Create the sub-documents as you can, even if they are blank. The sub-documents should all use the same template. You can create master documents from sub-documents with different templates, but you might have formatting problems.

2 Use the same template to create the master document. Click FILE > SEND > CREATE MASTER DOCUMENT and save. You can use a blank document, or a sub-document. If you use a sub-document, then it will be first in the master document, and will not be deletable.

Tip

Master documents all have an .odm extension. However, you can start the name with "master-document" for quicker identification, at least while you are working.

Caution

Unless your default template is the one that the master document uses, do not create a master document from FILE > NEW > MASTER DOCUMENT. You want to ensure that you are dealing only with the template you want.

Unless the master document and sub-documents share the same template, the sub-documents reformat each time you use the master document, increasing the chances of corruption.

3   The Navigator is open when you finish saving the master document. Use its features to add and position all the sub-documents (as described above).

4   Add any tables of contents, indexes, and bibliographies directly to the master document when all the sub-documents are complete.

Adding cross-references between sub-documents

Adding cross-references between two sub-documents in a master documents is similar to adding a cross-reference in another document. However, because headings do not display, you must set references manually, in an awkward work-around:

1 Open the sub-document you plan to reference (the source document). You can open it by itself, or from the master document.

2 Highlight the text for the reference, and click INSERT > CROSS-REFERENCE > SET REFERENCE.

   The FIELDS dialog window opens to the CROSS-REFERENCES tab. The selected text is entered in the VALUE field.

3 Enter a name for the reference. Then click the INSERT button. In the text, the selected text now has the gray shading that marks a field.

   Choose a name that is unique not only in the current sub-document, but all other sub-documents. The easiest way to ensure uniqueness is to make the name and the value identical. You can also keep a separate note of each name in a spreadsheet.

   ## Tip
   To view the reference, change to the Navigator's view of the master document and look under REFERENCES.

4 Save the source sub-document with the reference.

5 Open the target document and select INSERT > CROSS REFERENCES > INSERT REFERENCE.

6 The FIELDS dialog window opens to the CROSS-REFERENCES tab.

Caution

Because the reference is in another document, it is not listed in the SELECTION pane.

7 Type the reference's NAME in the target document.

8 Make a selection from the INSERT REFERENCE TO pane. CHAPTER is the chapter number, REFERENCE the text of the reference.

9 In the target document, enter the lead text, then select the format followed by the INSERT button.

Because the target sub-document cannot find the reference in the source sub-document, the message ERROR: REFERENCE SOURCE NOT FOUND displays.

Caution

This error message may cause problems with pagination when the sub-document is open by itself. You can ignore the problems if the sub-document is only going to be used in the master document.

10 Save the target sub-document with the cross-reference. When you re-open the master document, it will be able to locate the reference, and the cross-reference will now display instead of the error message. Pagination problems due to the error message are also corrected.

If you open the sub-document with the cross-reference from outside the master document, the cross-reference fields show the error message again.

STOP Caution

Cross-references are based on the names of sub-documents. If you change a sub-document's name – for instance, to indicate a draft – you have to re-insert any cross-references to it.

Moving beyond basics

By this point, the importance of styles should be proved beyond any doubt. When you do not use styles, you waste time and limit your possible actions. It's that simple.

In the next four excerpts from *Designing with LibreOffice*, you can learn the details of using styles in Writer, Calc, Draw, and Impress, the four main modules of LibreOffice.

Index

A

alphabetical index 79
AMA citations 99
AMA format 97, 99
APA citations 99
APA format 97, 98
automatic styles 24
automating style application
39
AutoUpdate 37

B

bibliographic formats 96
bibliographies 92

C

cell styles 21
character styles 20
Chicago format 97, 98
citations 92
concordance 90
creating styles 36
cross-referencing
   in one document 75
   to another file 77
custom styles 24, 26

D

date and time fields 60
default styles 28
deleting styles 38
Designing with LibreOffice 10
direct formatting 11
documents
   linking with templates 44

E

endnotes 100

F

fields in templates 60
file manager, templates in 67
Fill Format mode 33
footnotes 100
Formatting tool bar 32
frame styles 20
FrameMaker 19

G

graphic styles 21

www.ingramcontent.com/pod-product-compliance
Lightning Source LLC
Chambersburg PA
CBHW031948190326
41519CB00007B/721